ARRIVAL PRESS

LISTENING LINES

Edited

By

SUZY GOODALL

First published in Great Britain in 1995 by
ARRIVAL PRESS
1 - 2 Wainman Road, Woodston,
Peterborough, PE2 7BU

SB ISBN 1 85786 371 2

FOREWORD

On 2 November 1995, The Samaritans are launching 0345 90 90 90 - a universal telephone number for the UK. This is the greatest innovation since the founding of the movement over 40 years ago. Since 1953, when our founder Chad Varah launched the service, we have evolved into a nationwide charity with over 200 Branches.

Now, with the advent of an easy-to-remember, single, national 'phone number, people in crisis can reach our service with greater ease. Like 999, 0345 90 90 90 will become another 'phone number that people will remember in times of crisis. When someone dials 0345 90 90 90 their call will be sent to a nearby Branch. It is undoubtedly an innovation to celebrate.

This poetry anthology is also a celebration; a celebration of the widening of availability and knowledge of our service through the One Number. However, although the number is new, the service remains the same. Samaritans volunteers will continue to offer the caller unconditional time and space in which to explore their emotions without judgement. The importance of talking about feelings, however dark and difficult to articulate, can never be underestimated. Just by talking about extreme feelings and finding that someone cares enough to listen can mean the difference between life and death. The Samaritans can, at times, literally be a lifeline.

This anthology evolved from an invitation to our 22,350 volunteers to write about their own feelings. The volume and variety of submissions was overwhelming. The following selected poems provide a down-to-earth insight into Samaritan experience; poems lyrical, and sometimes humorous, about the highs and sadnesses of being a Samaritan. At times, a unique connection is made between strangers.

I should emphasise that confidentiality is a fundamental principle of The Samaritans, and has been maintained throughout this book as in everything else we do.

Jenny Cunnington
Chairman, The Samaritans
September 1995

THE SAMARITANS

The Samaritans is a nationwide charity, founded in 1953, which exists to provide confidential emotional support to any person, irrespective of race, creed, age or status, who is suicidal or despairing; and to increase public awareness of suicidal feelings.

The need for The Samaritans is clear from the statistics. Every two hours, someone in the UK dies by suicide. Every two minutes, it is estimated that someone attempts to take their own life. The rate of suicide is rising, especially amongst men, who are now four times more likely than women to kill themselves.

In 1994, The Samaritans received 3.75m contacts; a call every nine seconds. Over the last decade, the number of calls to the service has increased by nearly a third. 94% of contacts are made by 'phone. The rest are by letter, e-mail, visits to Branches, prison support and face-to-face contacts at festivals.

To maintain The Samaritans' service, in order to meet this need, requires £5m per annum. The Samaritans is a charity in need of funds to train its volunteers, maintain its Branches and for the essential promotion of its service. Only 9% of the charity's income comes from the Government. The rest is dependent on the generosity of companies, trusts and the general public. In addition, The Samaritans always needs more volunteers in order to keep the service available 24 hours a day, 365 per year.

The Samaritans is a volunteer-led movement with a vision: That fewer people will take their own lives because Samaritan befriending is always available at any hour, day or night, for everyone passing through personal crisis and at risk of suicide. The Samaritans provide society with a better understanding of suicide, suicidal behaviour and the value of expressing feelings that may lead to suicide. By this, The Samaritans confront the taboo that still surrounds suicide in our society.

If you wish to make a donation to The Samaritans or would like further information about their work, please contact the General Office of The Samaritans, 10 The Grove, Slough SL1 1QP Tel: 01753 - 532713 Fax: 01753 -

819004. If you are interested in becoming a listening or fundraising volunteer please contact your local Branch (details in the 'phone book).

Listening Lines

This celebratory anthology of Samaritans' poetry has been compiled by Sheila Coggrave, former Chairman of The Samaritans. Without her, and Arrival Press, the Samaritans' voices which follow would still be silent and unpublished.

CONTENTS

EVER SINCE I HAD ME OP

Hello, it's nice to see you looking well,
What? How am I?
I haven't been so good myself
But I've been getting by
No, I've had a bit of trouble
Well, I wouldn't bore a friend
But if you knew how much I'd suffered
Well, your hair would stand on end.

No, I'm not one to complain
And we all have our cross to bear
And I wouldn't even tell you
What they did to me up there
If you asked how many stitches
I wouldn't let it cross me lips
Well alright then, twenty-seven
And that's not including clips.

Course, it was only fifty fifty
On the drip all night and day
Oh they gave me all the lot
And then they took it all away
You wouldn't have recognised me
And I'm glad I never seen ya
And the doctor on the case
Gave up and went back home. To Kenya.

Well, I know you're in a hurry
And you haven't time to stop
And I've just seen Deirdre
She'll want to know about me op
And there's always someone worse off
Than yourself, without a doubt,
In my case I haven't met him
But I'm sure that he's about.

And you're healthy dear, enjoy it
For it fades away so soon,
Now I've got me eighteen pills
So I'll get through this afternoon
Don't give a thought to how I've suffered
I'm the last one to complain
I'll just keep smiling through it all
Until we meet again.

Pam Ayres

FEELINGS

WHAT PRICE?

Corridors of despair,
Twisting winding stairs.
I can't escape!
My mouth's been taped.
My voice cut out,
A verbal drought.
Questions stacked,
My brain is wracked,
For answers lost,
There *is* a cost.

Nicky

WAITING FOR THE TRAIN

What would you do if you ran out of time
What would you do if you stepped on the line
What would you do if the train came on time
What would you do if you rang the Samaritan line.

Having a go may mean the end
Having a go may make you scared
Having a go may mean you bend
Making a call would show we cared.

Could that call help at all
Could that call help stop your fall
Could that call relieve you at all.

As a *Sam* I know it will
As a *Sam* I hope you call
As a *Sam* I will be your friend
To talk your troubles through before the end.

Adrian 123

MEASURE OF CONTENT

Encumbered limbs,
Where passing years have set
Their grip, though thoughts still fly,
The self unageing meets advancing age.

The years that brought
The sorrowing, the joys
Have chiselled dross and cleared
Some tempered depth, and yet impregnable.

That tempered depth
Contains, withstands and holds
The daily fight, the ache,
Loves precious bonds, forever tightening.

Yet now the search
For nature's peace; to feel
The earth, seed, leaf and sky
And intimations faint, discerned with hope

And so through this
A deeper calm to come,
Before not known, but felt
In rarer moments, when the clamour fades.

When nourished thus,
With distilled peace, the self
Can give; and through the years,
With peace bestowed, perhaps may peace bestow.

BWC

LONELINESS

We chose the house together,
(Far from former friends and grimy streets)
And revelled in its seclusion.
Listened to the lark at dawn,
Watched the blackbird with her brood,
Rejoiced in nature's bounty.

Now, my mate is dead,
Snatched out of time,
And I, the older one,
Am left,
Alone,
Isolated,
Floating on a sea of nothingness,
With no purpose in my life.

Visitors come,
Uttering comforting words,
'Time heals all'.
Their duty done,
They leave.
The door slams.

The house echoes with emptiness,
And I could scream with weariness.
But there's nobody here
To care.

Nancy (Lowestoft)

A FRESH START

My life began in a small flat,
A bed, some chairs, a small round mat,
Ma did her best but couldn't cope,
By five or six I had no hope.

Social Services performed their role,
Got me fostered, found a school,
New Aunts and Uncles - all of them tried,
But something deep inside had died.

At fourteen I left and ran away,
I couldn't face another day,
My friends were dropouts, selfish yet 'free',
But I longed for one to listen to *me*.

I begged and borrowed, sometimes stole,
To get my food and smokes and coal,
I wished my misery would end,
Yet never had just one true friend.

Life was so empty - I wished I'd died,
Wanted to run - nowhere to hide,
No one to talk to, no one to care,
Wanted someone with whom to share.

Didn't want to live, didn't want to think,
No comfort found in sex, drugs or drink,
One day a sign, pasted up - brand new,
Samaritans listen - do you?

A chat or two, some cups of tea,
Someone at last who'd listen to *me*
Picked up the pieces, made a fresh start,
Thank you for being there and giving me heart.

Trevor Macey

LISTEN, I'M A CALLER

Dear Sams, Oh I am tired, as I wend my weary way,
Among life's fears and troubles, in my complicated day.
Just listen

My message is so simple, to open souls like yours,
I wish to just unburden, my love and grief and sores,
Please listen

Mountains are like molehills, they seldom disappear,
Exaggerated problems, that sometimes cost us dear.
Just listen

Ever had a restless night, events with no solution?
A call to you is worth a lot, it helps my resolution.
Please listen

Just a kid with childish views, friend's dare to me is heeded,
Please understand the urge to call, one day you may be needed.
Just listen

Addicts and addictions, what starts us down that road?
Experimental pastime, with mysteries to unfold.
Please listen

Children not a burden, I know it should be true,
But please do not despise me, when I slander them to you.
Just listen

Relationships are costly, to those who love just misses,
Phonecalls give some comfort, instead of kissed and kisses.
Please listen

I telephoned but panicked, when his voice I heard,
A lady was my object, a talk, a sigh, a word.
Just listen

Marriage is a lovely thing, its high spots all requited,
Give me time to tell you why, the ideal match is blighted.
Please listen

I have a fear of silence, my partner's time has come,
Death seems just so final, after many years of none.
Just listen

Suicidal leanings, at home and when I'm walking?
Help me cope with darkened clouds, by seeing through my talking.
Please listen

Fear of that awful news, the terminal diseases,
Is often muted calling you, dread it just decreases.
Just listen

Thank you all for patience, when dealing with our needs,
Confidences guarded, not harshly judging deeds.
Did you hear?

Ray 110

WHO'S CALLING?

You can call them through the night, call them through the day
'Samaritans, Can I help you?' Is what they always say

Help me I want to live, help me I want to die
Stay with me and listen, listen while I cry

I'm broke, my partner's dying, I'm lost can't find my way
Now that I have called I don't know what to say

I'm lonely, I've got friends, I'm depressed, I'm feeling fine
Are you there? Will you listen? On the end of the line

Who are the listeners waiting out of sight?
What type of person calls them in the night

The answer to both questions is simple, can't you see?
The caller and the listener, well they're just you and me.

Peter

UNTITLED

The time, the place, who gives a damn!
I am just a woman you're typical Sam!
I can take on hurt, but never become,
As bitter and twisted as I see some,
So carry your troubles till the load's too heavy,
Or ring and chat to help even the levy.
Whatever shall happen we always remain,
A listening ear to help ease the pain.

Time it's passing still I don't see.
Why is it the past can't set me free.

Carole

UNTITLED

Are you there?
In the silence of the night
A lonely heart calls out
Needing the sound of a friendly voice
Are you there?

Are you there?
While we grieve
Needing comfort, strength and love,
Just to go on -
Are you there?

I am here
With listening heart,
Lightening the darkness,
Offering hope, with the dawn,
I am here.

Anne

UNTITLED

He comes again,
Same life, same story,
Same despair.

Happy now,
No more strife.
He takes his life.

Trixie

SO ALONE

There is nobody out there,
At 4.30 am.
My reflection,
A hostile stranger,
Stares through me,
From a black window pane.

I'm the only person,
Alive, barely
In the world.
So cold, so alone,
Searching,
For somewhere to turn.

I pick up the telephone,
Desperate for someone to hear,
It rings, just three times,
And a voice reaches out,
Through my darkness.
Gripping the receiver, I sob with relief.

Agnes

LISTENING

We sit there waiting
Passing the time.
Some knit, some talk,
Some read, some think.
But all just waiting
For the phone or doorbell to ring.
When it does, we jump.
Not upright, but the heart misses a beat.
You go to the door with a smile
Or pick up the phone.
'Hello, Samaritans, May I help you?'
It's time to listen.

We sit there listening
Face to face or on the phone.
Sometimes the voice is strong,
So what is wrong?
Sometimes the sobs,
So what is wrong?
'My name is Bill.
Do you want to talk.
I'm here for you, willing to listen.'

Listen we do.
Face to face or on the phone.
No one need to be on their own.
Samaritans are here for one and all,
No one need be on their own.
We listen to the good and bad calls.
Yes, we listen,
We will always listen.

Taffy

THE BOY

The boy alone, he sings from the heart,
The boy alone, awaits a new start
His family departed, to heaven he prays
The boy in the orphanage lives in dismay
The boy is wanted a couple have come
To take him away to become their son.
The boy is happy, he now sings out loud
No more is his life hidden under a dark cloud.

Christine M

THE SAMARITANS. A VOLUNTEER

I am just a volunteer
Who likes to give a listening ear
To anyone who has a problem a worry
Or a fear.

When people are suicidal
And need someone to share
I only want to be there
Because I really care.

I cannot give advice
No matter how I am asked to try
Sometimes I feel sad
And I feel the need to cry.

I am just an ordinary person
With ordinary feelings too
A volunteer Samaritan
Who really cares for you.

Ruth (Inverclyde)

THE END OF THE ROAD

'Hello Samaritans can I help you?' I say
'I don't know where to begin.'
'Take your time it's okay.'

'I've had a terrible day,
Things are getting bad.
I've come to the end of the road.
It'll soon be over and I'm glad.'

'You say you have taken tablets,
You intend to die.'
I tell you you are not alone.
Then I hear you cry.

'Would you like someone with you?
One of us will come to you.'
'No!' You say. 'Just talk to me.
That's all I want to do.'

So I listen,
And my heart goes out to you.
I repeat.
'Are you sure this is what you want to do?'

I listen to your story,
And respect your decision,
Your choice.

Then gradually,
I can no longer hear your voice.
'Hello!' I say
'Can you hear me,
I am still here?'

Only your shallow breathing
I hear in my ear.
As time goes on
Not a sound can I hear.

You have done what you wanted.
Just as you made clear.
Then I put the phone down,
And wipe away a tear.

Lara

COMMUNITY CARE

Our welcome smile fades away
When he stands at the door.
No longer can he come in here
As he did before.

There are too many now,
For us to care about.
The hospitals are closing down,
And they are being let out.

Pausing for a moment
As if to say goodbye,
He slowly turns back down the road,
And with a silent cry
Collapses in a doorway
With nowhere left to hide
People rushing past him
He commits suicide.

Soon he lies forgotten
In a pauper's grave,
This unimportant lonely man
Whose life we could not save.

Marion

YES, OF COURSE

A school talk?
        Yes, of course.
When can we come?
        That's fine.
Always pleased to do them
        Anytime.

We're on our way. How will it go?
We've not been there before.
Will they listen or fidget, or gaze through the window?
        I wish it were over.

We're running late. Where is the place?
We've not been there before.
Let's hope the video works, and the teacher supports us.
        Why do we do it?

Relax . . . deep breaths.

Will they ask questions - will they take part?
We've not been there before.
A difficult age, sullen, bored, looking at watches.
        Why did I come?

We're introduced and on our own.
It goes OK - not good, not bad, but no hitches.
They seem to listen, they like the video,
But there's no questions, no feedback, no response.
The painter at the window didn't help
And the teacher marked her books.
Anyway it's over, we've done our best.
Schools talks are not for me. I'll not come again.

By the door, fumbling in her bag, a girl hangs back,
Looking but not looking,
Can I talk to you, please?
        Yes, of course.

Yes, of course - and of course I'll come again
And of course I'll do it again.
Of course I'll still feel the same, but I'll be there.
Because - one never knows . . .

Meg

TORN WINGS

With barbed criticism in your eyes and
Jagged assault on your tongue
You snared my childhood and
Left me limping through life.

Sheltering under bruised skies,
My shadows drowning in
Puddles of insignificance,
I trapped nuances under misted jars,
Picked at sore enemies,
Gambled with grey strips of days,
Peeled the dried stains from yesterday's face.

All the time despising your cool lake of nothingness;
Memories floating in buoyant tranquillity.

I understand torn wings can fly.

I found myself bathing his wrinkled mind
With long sunny days.
Anger hammered down into a waiting silence.
Broken glass swept away.

Eve

TURNING POINT

Turn distress and sorrow into strength.
Turn anger, irritation and disappointment into searching;
Be content with a share of living and,
When autumn has passed, the life force will awake
for the second time, this one spring day.

Christine

ALIVE AGAIN

No one can take the heartache away,
Or the pressure inside your head,
The numbness, when all hope is dead,
And you wish you were dead instead,
But know that you have to stay.

Days are endless; black gaping pits,
You topple in and down, down you go,
Each memory hits you, like a blow,
The whole world seems to go so slow,
And the future is in a thousand bits.

You have no strength to rise above,
The sheer blankness in your mind,
Cobwebs round each thought wind,
Understanding is very hard to find,
But harder to find is self love.

Then one day, though still in pain,
You hear a solitary bird sing,
Or feel the warmth sun can bring,
Or see new buds just opening,
And know that you're alive again.

Alice Skeet

HOPE

Despairingly, despairingly -
I weep and stray alone and cry,
I seek a way of ending my
Life just because girls always shy
Afar away - beyond from me.

Despairingly, despairingly -
I howl from in my heart that bleeds,
I tread this wide expanse of weeds,
I retch in wretchedness that feeds
On lovelorn-ness and misery.

Despairingly, despairingly -
I sigh so sorrowful and sick,
Lost in this dreary wasteland thick
With brambles that profusely prick
On every single part of me.

Despairingly, despairingly -
Down-sunk to such a lowly pitch -
I plod and plunge into a ditch
Of nasty nettles all of which
Stab stinging pains all over me.

I screech and scramble here and scream,
I lie alone, bruised, cut and cold,
I look, but then my eyes behold
One early daffodil of gold -
Emitting such a joyous gleam.

Now happily, now happily -
I rise and see the bloom foretell
How everything shall hence be well
Because a girl will someday dwell
In love forevermore with me.

Robert

PAIN

And
Pain again -
again
and again -
this awful pain.

Oh, Jesus, I wish
that I had never
been born,

My dear, no wonder
The wound in my side
Is still torn.

I share your pain
Again and again.

It would be good
If that were something
Understood.

Anne Shells

UNTITLED

What do I do, where do I turn,
To understand this mess I yearn,
Family and friends I cannot tell,
The pain and anguish make me want to yell.

What do I do, where do I turn,
Lessons from this I want to learn,
Who can help me to understand . . .
Why not try a Samaritan.

Denise

THERE'S SOMEONE TO CARE

Don't worry! Don't be afraid!
There's someone to listen!
There's someone to care!

When life's a real downer
You're not all alone!
You can't talk to your family
You're still not alone!
Your friends are too busy
But some friends do care!

Don't worry! Don't be afraid!
There's someone to listen!
There's someone to care!

Just pick up the phone
You're not alone!
You don't have to talk
You just know someone's there!
When you're afraid and alone
There's someone to care!

Don't worry! Don't be afraid!
There's someone to listen!
There's someone to care!

Patricia

UNTITLED

'Hello - Samaritans - can I help you?'
She sobs quietly, and I wait,
straining to hear - did she say something?
'I'd like to help, if you think you can talk to me . . . ?'
Again - silence.
Then more sobbing - piteous, heart-rending tears.
I tell her my name, and gently comment,
(stating the obvious?)
that she sounds terribly distressed -
can she tell me why?
Silence. Then suddenly,
I get the feeling that I'm losing her,
and I want to plead with her;
'Don't go - please speak to me'
but then, why should she?
It's her choice, I know -
and perhaps she feels it's enough, for now,
just to know that we're here?
But I still feel, somehow,
that I may have failed her,
as she sobs one last time
and replaces the receiver.

Lesley

COLLECTION

Saturday - and Richmond Tube
Crowded with a lunchtime throng
Rugby players in search of ale
For Twickenham - their Mecca ground.

What a sight whilst standing there
With a tin for charity
Fans arriving sporting flowers
Daffodils and emblems weird.

For this was tribalistic game
English versus Celtic Welsh
Harking back to mists of time
Henry Hotspur - Glendower bold.

An in the midst of seething mass
Pause - reflect - and gather thoughts
People gave so generously
A quiet word - a listening ear.

For this is what we are to those
In despair - a life-line link
A helping hand in troubled world
Proud to be Samaritan.

Steve

UNTITLED

I'm glad you called, a difficult choice
I feel your pain, as a physical touch
together we drift thro' your levels of sadness
and there with an intimacy quickly forged
tarry a while, to stroll among your losses
that swirl round us like dried autumn leaves.

And now you are gone my brief companion
the choice was your own to make.
And though I may never speak to you again
I shall bear a small part of you in my soul,
And as I sit reflecting. I shall think of you
but now I rise again to the bell, and say
Samaritans, can I help you?

Keith

HELP ME

My problem is so big so heavy
I am sinking, being pushed down
By forces that possess and depress
That smother and stifle
From this anguish I call
Then hang up.
I call again
And again
Are you listening?
Yes you really are listening
Someone is listening to me.

Mary

FORTY MINUTES

Did it help?
Did it really help?
Forty minutes - are you suicidal?
Unsure, uncertain, left behind by life,
your pain seized me but did I share
your torment? Perhaps - perhaps not.
Perhaps I'm not to know - just wonder
where and how you are, and were you suicidal?
We shared some space, some time, perhaps some hope,
I gave you what I could - some forty minutes - just.
You gave me all you had, you gave your trust.

Bill 46 (Canterbury)

I WENT TO HIS FUNERAL

He wanted to die,
Oh, how he wanted to die
For many long years he wanted to die.

He tried, oh how he tried,
But he lived, he talked, and then he died.

A Samaritan listened, two Samaritans listened,
for Five long years support was given.

His poetry was beautiful,
His music divine,
His talent prolific,
His feelings benign.

He lived and loved,
He suffered . . . He overdosed and died.

I went to his funeral - and I cried.

Audrey

THAT PLAINTIVE VOICE

I sit and stare at the telephone,
There's someone there who's all alone.

The story's old - the story's new
How do I know if it's false or true.

So many thoughts within my head,
So many lives hang by a thread,
But then I hear that lonesome cry
'I really really want to die
I cannot face another day
I simply want to fade away.'

That plaintive voice within the night
That gave me such a shivering fright.

And then his story does unfold,
How life is bad - it's cruel - it's cold.
He said he has 'just one last aim,
To play no more the living game.'

So I keep him on the phone
And tell him that he's not alone,
I tell him that I really care,
And how I feel his sad despair.

But then he went just as he came,
I did not even know his name.

That plaintive voice within the night
That gave me such a shivering fright.

I breathe in deep - and then I sigh,
So many people want to die,
I sit and stare at the telephone,
There's someone there who's all alone.

Stephen George Owen

LIVE FOR US

Oh, sweet babe, why so sad,
you really think the world so bad?
It's hard to know your pain,
but we all know what it's like
To be in the rain.

It's difficult to know what to say,
to settle your mind, to live another day,
Life is so good, when you look at the sky,
to see the sun beaming, it reflects in your eye,
Let it reflect the warmth, the warmth in my heart,
To cuddle you and keep you, quite safe in life's hearth.

Watch the birds that fly, they soar aloft, so high,
with a song in their heart, they whistle their tune,
So high, so very high, to their God in the sky.

Let the sun's warmth heal you,
You owe us a chance,
To show you we love you,
And teach you to dance.

Helen Selwood

BAD NEWS DAY

I tried to reassure her
That it needn't be the end.
That on life's long and winding trail
She'd only reached a bend.

Then in Friday's newspaper
I read that she had died.
And for this lonely, unloved soul
I went upstairs and cried.

George

STEP BY STEP

With each unsteady step
I wonder
Why here?
Where next?
And what for?

Then finding distractions
The panic subsides

All seems fit
To build upon:
A kind of home.

Before long
Boredom, nostalgia
Uneasiness
Ensue,
Feet, never firmly
Set . . .
Now aching to move
On

And then
I wonder
Why?
Where?
And what for?

Driven by nothing it seems
But the fears
Inside.
Of failure, growing old
And death . . .
Fears of others
And of myself
. . . Fears of life
Fears which demand

The next unsteady step.

One day, there'll be nowhere
Left to go.
What then?

S Greaves

SILENT TELEPHONE

'Nothing more we can do'
the doctor said, shrugged his shoulders,
yet another suicide statistic;
he'd become immune over the years
to blood and sorrow, death and tears.

She had been thirty years old
had her share of pain and pleasure
the latest lover, the hardest to lose:
too many words were left unsaid
too many tears already shed.

'We must give her a call'
all her friends had said,
when we can, when we're not so busy,
we told her we've got our own lives too,
'We can't always be there for you.'

A lethal cocktail of booze and pills,
she'd sat in the darkened room,
tablets held in her shaking hand,
hoping the phone would ring maybe one more time -
it could have been a positive sign.

So she had died, alone and cold,
lying on the bed, full make-up on,
best dress to look good for this final scene;
she'd torn up her suicide note -
there'd be no-one around to care what she wrote.

Sue

THE TIN-MAN

I wish I were a tin-man,
All smooth and shining bright;
I'd work just like a robot
From morning until night.

I would whistle tinny tunes
As the busy day flew by,
With, stamped upon my shining rim,
The words 'Arbeit macht frei'.

I'd dust and sweep and scrub and clean
Each cranny, nook and stair,
And when I found the bottles - why!
I wouldn't turn a hair.

No anxiety, no searing pain
Would stab me in the chest
I'd grasp them with my tin-man hands
And put them with the rest.

And when, at night, you don't come home,
I'd lie upon my bed,
Dreaming dreams that Tin-men dream,
Inside my hollow head

The nightmare comes - my tin dissolves,
I'm flesh and blood once more.
Exposed, betrayed - and patiently,
Death's waiting at the door.

Sophie

HOPE

'How do you feel?' the Samaritan said
I cried as I told her, my baby's not fed,
Did she honestly care that I was unwed,
Unable to cope with what lay ahead?

'How do you feel?' came the soft reply,
Did she care that my lover was passing me by?
With a couple of drinks I'd feel quite high
I'd feed my baby, by and by.

'How do you feel?' she asked me again
Did she not know I must be insane
The cries of hunger coming from my wean
Only added a lot to my pain.

'How do you feel?' I heard her say
As moments of darkness gave way to day
'I must feed my baby', I heard myself say
'I'll talk to you later, don't go away'.

'How do *you* feel?' darling baby of mine
TLC came from Mary will also be thine
You and I baby are going to be fine.
We'll call Mary to tell her at half past nine.

Kate

BEING THERE

I often sit and ponder
On all the things I am
A daughter, wife, a mother
And also I'm a *Sam*
My life is never mundane
Sometimes I'm in a lather
But when speaking with a caller
All my senses I must gather
To help a fellow being
In his sorrow and distress
To listen without judging
Or advising what is best
To help him tell his problem
And express his inner fears
To tell him I am there to share
His sadness and his tears
Then later in the contact
When anxieties subside
Comes the most important question
Have you thoughts of suicide
And although we're not *Samaritans*
For personal gain or glory
I feel deep satisfaction
When he thanks me for my care
and says -
'Not now, it's helped to talk, and
thanks for *being there'*

Val (Plymouth)

THREE LITTLE RINGS

Ring-ring, ring-ring, ring, ring
That instant trigger to the mind,
Mid-sentence, before the punch-line
Steaming coffee left behind.
Silence, breathing, sobbing,
A cry for help before the crash.

What privileged being am I?
That others open their hearts and tell,
Their thoughts, their feelings, their private hell?
Oh, that I should be worthy of such faith
To wave a magic wand and make all well.

Alas, for some, no wand could work so.
Despair, confusion, pain and darkness,
When death seems sweet, a rosy glow,
But fear of crossing that final hurdle,
Prolongs the suffering, defeats the goal,
And corsets the bowel like a sickening girdle.
We can but listen; share a little,
The anguish of that poor demented soul.

Yet for others, a listening ear, encouraging word,
Calms the brow, unravels the turmoil.
The sobbing stops, coherence reigns.
Sharing, healing, soothing oil.
A word of thanks, a spoken smile,
Such wealth brings, that spurs us on,
Ever ready for those three little rings.

Terry Sweeney

CALLER

You reach out
I am there
to hold your hand
and show care
whether
you decide
to go ahead
with suicide
or change
your mind
to live your life
I will remain
with you

My only thought
is for you
not what
you ought to do.
Talking
may ease the pain
and sometimes
a light might flame
where there was
none before

Majella

YESTERDAY TODAY TOMORROW

Why do I sit here and look towards the phone
Maybe for once you are not at home.
Many a time I sit curled up in this chair,
Today I am wondering if you will be there.
Glance up at the clock it is almost upon nine,
The telephone is ringing, is that you on the line.
Your voice is unsteady not very clear,
I reach out to assure you it's okay I am here.
Rain upon the window sliding down like your tears,
If only a magic wand could wipe away those fears.
Always remember you are never really alone,
Just ring this number some one is always at home.
Please be warmed a little with a sound of a voice
If you cannot talk now that is fine, your choice.
Time to go now I yawn and ruff my hair,
Some one else is sitting in that warm cosy chair.
At times when you feel you cannot get through
Remember dial, 'Samaritans can I help you?'

Sue

PAIN

It is really the frustration that hurts so much.
I know that I am not functioning well.
I find it very difficult.
You want blood. Too much has been spilt.
Vulnerable and very unsure of those who are not.
When will it stop?
Despite my craft I run out of words.
I need to cry or die.
Tomorrow maybe. Today I suffer.

Mark

TRANSITIONS

Once, we had an office, now
It's a centre,
Which means I suppose we have to be careful
Not to assume
That we're all in the middle
While they're all on the margins.

Once, we had clients, now
They are callers,
Which means I suppose we have to be conscious
That if we had their number
And half their problems
We could be calling them.

Once, we were people, now
We're Samaritans,
Which means I suppose we have to be careful
When we go out from the centre
Into the world of callers
That we become people again.

Or have we?

Michael

RING RING

Today, death came over the phone
As she listened to grief in a man all alone
Bereft, he said in a voice choked with tears
He had just buried his wife of 30 years
A wonderful woman - a wonderful wife
What could he do with the rest of his life.
Out poured that age old call
'What is the point of life, who cares at all?

In the still of the night she quietly replied
I care, I am here, hold my hand
I know you are hurting, I know there is pain
We will always listen, we will always care
There is no problem you cannot share
'You are very kind' the sad voice said
'A new day is dawning and I'll go to bed'
He put down the phone and the line went dead.

She replaced her receiver with a troubled face
Had she done enough, had she shown she cared?
Her friend came over and gave her a hug
And said with a voice full of tender love
I will listen, I will care.
Don't think for *you* there is no one there
He may ring again, he knows we are here
And whatever else, he has our ear.

Jill

TWENTY TO THREE IN THE MORNING

Twenty to three in the morning
And the lights go on again
However I try, the sleep won't come
Going over and over the pain.

I've friends to talk to through the day
Friends who always listen
But somehow it's never quite the same
There's always something missing.

I saw your advert - but not for me
I'm not lonely - just a little bit sad
I've loads of things to be grateful for
. . . So why do I feel so bad?

Maybe I'll ring, just for a while
To give those friends a rest
From me going over and over my woes
Wondering what to do for the best.

'Samaritans . . . Can I help you?
Snap - The phone goes down
You sounded kind, it made me cry
Always the tears of a clown.

'Samaritans . . . Can I help you?'
I don't know where to start
I've lots of things to be grateful for
. . . But I've got a broken heart.

I tell you things I'd never ever
Dream of telling friends.
You listen - never judging
Until my story ends.

Do you ever think of suicide?
I'm shocked - how could you know
But the relief I feel in saying . . . Yes!
You'll never ever know.

After that night, it seemed to change
But I phoned for nights on end
At twenty to three in the morning
To my faceless anonymous friends.

The years went by and I got strong
What could I do where I'd really belong
French or German - Spanish or Greek?
Flower arranging or mending a leak?

I saw your advert - but not for me.
I was sure you'd turn me down.
'Samaritans . . . Can I help you?'
Snap - The phone went down.

'Samaritans . . . Can I help you?'
I'd like to help out if I could
But I'm only a normal person
I don't know if I'd be any good.

You see we're all *normal* people
To listen and comfort and care
Whatever the problem, how big or how small
There will always be somebody there.

Twenty to three in the morning
Awakening me with a start
'Samaritans . . . Can I help you?'
Yes . . . I've got a broken heart.

Mandy

SAM'S SONG

Driving through the sunlit meadows,
Cosy houses, smiling day.
When I reach the friendly centre
My own troubles fade away.

Kindly chatter, kettle boiling,
Several calls, some sad, some blue.
Then the desperate, weeping whisper:
'Help me please, what can I do?'

Secretly the doubts invade me,
Can I hold this fragile contact?
Listening, caring, being with her,
Hearing what her life has lacked.

Leaving now, into the darkness,
Echoes of the weeping girl
In my mind are fading slowly
As the homeward miles unfurl.

Averil

DESIRE

A man desires a woman, a man desires a man.
A woman desires a woman, a woman desires a man.
Which desire does not matter when you're on the phone,
For they all have a problem and all have a soul.

They're genuine people, some hurt, grieved or sore
For the way they've been treated or cheated or more.

But one thing is certain, when phoning is done,
The duty all finished, new friendships won.
If we think we are better than those on the phone
Then simply get up, pack up and quietly go home.

Dave

WHAT HAS BEING A SAMARITAN DONE FOR ME

My own life took a turning point,
My body was no longer fit for work.

My soul still had a strong will to carry on, and feel empathy
for my fellow person's hurt!

I trained as a Samaritan *volunteer,*
and questioned myself, could I really put my listening skills
to, suicide, rape, loneliness, despair, anger, and fear!

Could I be none judgmental to the caller with - Aids, or a
Homosexual, an Alcoholic, a violent person, a child abuser, *And* . . .

Well I certainly would-not judge what I don't *understand!*

Sams do not opinionate, judge or condone!
We offer support to those in their time of feeling, hurt, lost,
and, most *alone!*

What has being a Samaritan done for Me?

There were times when I felt down,
For silly things I used to worry, witter, and *moan!*

Now I feel I belong, I am somebody! I am that caring, listening
person at the end of the *phone!*

Debbie 118

SUSAN - COULD BE HER NAME

She bent down slowly to sit in the chair,
Heavy bodied, ungainly, unfit. Her hair
Like a curtain, so thick, strong and brown,
Large arms gently covered in childlike down,
Yet ribbed with scars from a razor so sharp,
Cut with eyes open, for fear of the dark
And fear of her thoughts and fear of dying
'What's the point?' she cries, then starts her crying.
Do I touch her and hug that big dark brown form?
She's no-one I know, yet I've known that same thorn,
That can pierce one's being, destroy one's state,
Turning balance and reason into rivers of hate,
But clouds on a hilltop do finally lift,
Leaving life's fine purpose no longer adrift.
But Susan sits, sobs, suffers and shakes,
What caused this pain which made her heart break?
Listening and talking to strangers who call,
Spilling secrets they usually tell to the wall,
Makes odd friendships, intense yet untried,
Such insight, such truth - we're newly allied.
Had Susan been nagged, or abused or thrashed?
Or was this another life-crisis crash?
To watch her in pain was awful to bear,
I carefully went and sat by her chair,
And placed my arm on her wide brown back,
And quietly stroked till the tension went slack.
Her heavy head fell, soft on my shoulder,
The crying abated . . . then the anger smouldered . . .
'I hate him, the bastard, he's cruel and despises
Whatever I've done, he just criticises,
Nothing I do for him is enough,
He's distant and cold, heartless and tough,
My mother given in, she always was weak,
My sister he loves - I'm just the freak.'
She lifts back her hair and gazes at me.
Eyes full of question - have I the key?

We talk and we listen together and share
The search for some tools to cope with despair.
There's no instant answer to cure her self-hate,
The clue is to live before it's too late
When the hate takes a grip and deadens all feeling
And care and respect seem to lose their whole meaning.
It seems to me after hundreds of calls,
And meetings with Susans, surrounded by walls,
That these moments of caring and intense quiet truth
Say more about love without needing the proof,
But finally, we are all on our own -
Unless and until you pick up the phone.

G 3640

WE DO THE BEST WE CAN

The necklace of river pearl coils in my hand.
Each stone is pressed with hollows and ridges.

It is a month since I looked at the moon,
Crescent and sharp. I can't say
'Beautiful', only take note
That one month has passed.

The white bone of your face across my lap
Has softened and flushed with warmth while you've slept.

When you wake your rage will sharpen to steel.
But in sleep, each sleep, I press
Hollows into your body. At dawn the frost
Will run pale mist along your ridges.

Imperfect stones link, moon by moon,
Stringing together some sort of life.

Jackie

42 ROSS STREET

When I was a courtier
I could write lines to break my heart.
With empathy in every pore
I felt connected to a stream of life
Disassociated, different, down
Underscored by pain of being
And there in almost every eye.

When I was a marriage ring
I could make my heart take flight
With words I placed betwixt - just so.
Belief was like a beacon then
Connected to a cosmic Love
And ever spinning webs to catch
The Moment fore it burst for good.

When I was a jaded loss
I barely ever wrote a thing.
Which lead me to believe it best
To connect myself, emotionally
To a garrett with a frugal view
Which, of course, did not work
For the music never ever stops.

When I was Paul 501
Which was, and is, through all of these,
I wondered if my heart were true
Or a mere reflection on my state.
So many words, and not one writ - cyphers for a life passed by?
And yet 'Samaritans, can I help you?'
Remains as meaningful and meant.

Paul

SAMS

I can't always remember what made me think I'd make a Sam
The reasons they don't matter, I'm just glad that I am,
I can't always agree with policies and today's current trends,
But the commitment goes on and just as strong in my friends
It never ceases to amaze me, we turn up night and day,
'I'm sure they must be crackers' I've even heard people say.
But there's something about being a Sam that stays in your soul
Not for us the high life or ambition our goal,
We don't even want recognition or payment for our time
Just the chance to maybe help and bring hope to your life and mine.

Vanessa

IS THERE A PLACE?

Is there a place where tranquillity lies?
Caught in a maelstrom of blistering pain
my soul hangs suspended,
pierced with arrows of hate and despair.
Ethereal shackles of self loathing bind my heart with grief.

Can blissful serenity ever prevail?
Cast adrift on a fathomless sea of desolation,
my sanity clings to the flotsam on the putrid foam.
Unrelenting waves of anger dash my shattered spirit
against rocks of pain.
Utter isolation haunts my tortured soul.

Where can my soul seek peaceful sanctuary?
My heart weeps desperate tears of sadness,
crying with a voice of anguish and fear.
Deliver me from my agony!
My being pleads for release and blessed oblivion.

Jean 787

THE EDGE

Pushed to the edge by the unseen other
I peer into the abyss.
Dark and deep, it beckons my rapid descent.
'Come to me my Brother,
Come to me my Sister,
I will hold you, and protect you,
and take away your pain.'

Peering down, tears fall
From the tip of my nose,
The tiny crystal waterfall
Diminishing into the dark.

The void calls to me again,
'Follow your tears. Be with me, be part of me.'

I turn, searching behind for a friend,
To tell goodbye, to tell I will be happy,
But instead another voice calls,
'I am here, I will listen, I will comfort you.
I judge nothing, I ask nothing,
Tell me your darkness,
So that together we many find your light.'

I turn back to the void,
'I may yet be back dear friend,
Yet just let me talk a little while'.

I turn once again, and move away from the edge.

Andy

ALL IN A SAM'S LIFE

In times before I was a Sam,
I thought I knew so many things
About the life that I had lived,
And each new day tomorrow brings.
That helped to make me who I am.
But how deficient was my ken,
Of all the myriad pains there are,
The loneliness, the cruel abuse
that go together; so to mar
Ones unrealistic thoughts of life.
How could one know the pressing need
At tether end, to take a call;
For verbal hands to hold, until
The self inflicted death, solves all
A selfish world declines to know.
Disturbing though it all can be.
And sometimes very hard to bear.
Without tranquillity, but yet
So thankful, yes, that I was there.

Stuart

BALANCE

Samaritans listen to troubles and woes,
And make cups of tea for our visitors, too.
Maybe you think that we're dull so-and-sos
And have to be solemn, all humour subdue?
Remove from your mind all such dolorous things!
In fact, we're as merry as merry can be
To balance the sorrows with which fortune stings,
And lighten the load of our colleagues when free.
No power can cure all life's ills, it is true,
So listen with love to those worse off than you.

Susanne

MY FIRST LOVE

I have loved you and been faithful to you,
you have been dead now many years
But my passion still burns on,
Why did you take your life my love,
You left an emptiness in my heart
If only I had been there for you.
Listened to you, but I did not understand,
how could I have changed anything
Why must I blame myself for your death
sometimes I want to join you.
But I have not got the courage.
I must wait to find the answers.

Brian

THE CALL

The Wise Men say 'Each moment Life's complete;
Three thousand worlds are in a moment's space'.
Philosophy? - yes, fine! a fit retreat
For dons, who, warm and snug with books, embrace
The sages' thoughts in peaceful contemplation.
But in despair the moment means defeat:
For well-turn'd texts don't offer consolation
To one bereft of friends, poor, hungry, cold;
Who invites Death, because there (only) lies
The way to numb'd oblivion; who cries
'There's nothing left for me, I'm all alone,
And yours the last restraining hand to hold -
Help me, you unknown voice on the telephone!'

Donald

THE STRANGER

A stranger walked along my street
and knocked upon my door
when the door was opened
I knew what he was asking for.

Food to warm his body
or coins to buy some bread
my heart filled up with sadness
but my mind filled up with dread.

I was alone with no-one near
no-one would hear my scream
what if this forlorn old man
was not what he would seem.

My logic of this sad sad world
made me turn away
hiding my fear behind the words
'Sorry, not today'.

He wandered off rejected
as I closed my door in shame
I hung my head in sorrow
as he returned from whence he came.

We see this stranger every day
in people that we meet
this stranger is our neighbour
for he lives on every street.

He lives within each person
from whom we turn away
hiding our fears behind the words
'Sorry, not today'.

Louise

TIES

Emotions rip
the unsuspecting grip
that holds the members close.
Family ties,
weakened by lies,
are powerless now;
except to bind.

What comfort, where,
what halt to this despair?
No peace, no rest,
no soft absorbing breast.

An end, a sleep,
that one eternal leap.
A drink, a pill
a fatal swill.
On to earthly end.

The die is cast;
and at the last,
sickening, cold, alone,
just me,
and a despairing telephone.

Norman

THE CALLER EXPLAINS

Now is my time of self destruction,
Of analysing my inadequacies,
Which are legion.
Each one must be examined separately
In excruciating detail;
Each one is damning in itself -
Together, they long ago cut me off
And left me stranded
On a private plane of desperation.

Tentatively
You reached out to touch me.
Instinctively
I backed away
Suspicious of your motivation.

Frightened again
I tried to crush my emotion -
To hold it under until it drowned.
But then, like the earth,
It erupted in another direction,
Smothering
Me again.

You, with your disturbing awareness,
Are part of the world that I want to be part of;
But my separateness excludes me again.

Jan 392 (Hereford)

UNTITLED

In despair
Who will be there?
The Samaritans
A kindly word
To tell you they care
A listening ear -
Who will be there?
The Samaritans
When you feel down
We will be found
A friend in the night
When all is quiet -
When feeling desperation
complete isolation
We will be there
For your moments of despair
Call us *The Samaritans*

Rosemary

THE CARERS

S ympathy and tea as well,
A ll are welcome here.
M any no place else to go,
A nd often shed a tear.
R igid we can never be
I n helping out a Caller.
T enderness, compassion too
A re what they need to savour.
N ever do we reprimand, and
S teadfast stays our little band.

Eleanor

LISTENING

So many people are blessed with the gift of hearing.
Our ears record the clamour of a busy city,
The gentler sounds of the countryside,
The ever-changing voice of the sea,
The laughter of children,
The roar of a crowd.
We hear words of love and sympathy, sorrow and joy
And share this gift with those around us.
Our ears absorb it all.
Our brains retain a small part of it.
We take it all for granted.
We can hear!
But do we listen?
Samaritans come from many different backgrounds, in all shapes and sizes.
We come with our own memories, preconceptions and experiences.
We have probably suffered some tragedy, loss or pain.
And our reasons for becoming Samaritans are also different
But rarely are they purely alatruistic.
In attempting to help others we, ourselves, find healing.
Not one of us is perfect.
We are all flawed.
Yet we are privileged.
Our callers trust us with their deepest fears, their pain and their despair.
They reveal to us what is hidden from those dearest to them.
So we have an obligation.
Not just to hear, but to listen.
Really listen - with our hearts.

Lisa

ANON

You must be very busy,
others trying to get through,
and it's only useless me,
but I'd like to talk to you.

I haven't telephoned before.
I'm going to kill myself today.
I'm absolutely sure.
There is nothing you can say.

You'd really like to know?
I don't know where to start.
Salty tears will flow,
you will hear a broken heart . . .

. . . I'm always such a bore,
the precious time has gone,
though there's so much more,
I've already stayed too long.

You care, you really care?
Well, thanks for listening, say,
are you still there?
Oh . . . maybe I won't - today.

Ken

LIFE

Let's face the task of real life,
You know the thing, that causes no strife
The one that never brings you pain,
The one that always keeps you sane
I'm sure you know just what I mean,
Of course you do, you've had the dream.

You've had the dream of perfect life,
The one that never causes strife.
The life that never brings you pain,
And yes the one that keeps you sane

But sometimes life don't go that way,
And all your dreams, just go astray,
When things just don't go as they should,
And you feel you've done all you could,
When all your problems tumble in,
And none of them you feel you'll win.

When you just feel you're on your own,
There is no one, you're all alone
No one to listen, no one to care,
No one to tell, why your life's so unfair.

At the end of the line you'll find a friend,
With plenty of time, and an ear to lend
Someone to listen, someone to care
Someone will always be there
No matter the time, no matter the day
There's always someone to hear what you say
Phone the Samaritans day or night
And tell us about your long hard fight.

Alison

AT LAST PEACE OF MIND

I want to know if it has happened to you or do you not have a clue where I am coming from. I sit and listen to friends chatting about the downs in life and remember what the downs to me really mean.

I still live with the strong memories of four years ago when my life was so sad. Not one person could have explained the deep inner feeling I was going to feel.

I was sitting in my mother's house on the floor looking at all my tablets and I was not frightened just numb inside.

I felt destroyed and so very much alone that no-one could help me. I didn't have time to think about the pain I would put my family through. The bitter anger was too strong, no feeling just numb. I felt my body was not mine, I was shaking from head to foot and sobbing.

Then I just stopped and looked into thin air, feeling happy with what I was doing, putting tablets, lots into my mouth to eat them. Then everything went black.

All I remember was the horror and stunned faces looking at me not understanding the pain I felt. As I wept my mother comforted me. I wanted to scream but I was still numb, not understanding why I was left to die like an animal in pain.

I can't forget, but I do care now about what I would have put my family through, and care that I am still here to tell the tale. I have learnt that people think that attempted suicide is something to be swept under the carpet but it is a cry for help.

You shouldn't think that you are weak or have done something wrong. It is up to the individual if you want your life or not. And I did, and learned to cope with the downs in life.

Jade

EASY

You know
it becomes easier
to stop crying
though the pain
is still there

We draw the curtains
on dark windows
remembering how much
we need the dreams

I sat with you
listening to your songs
in the comfortable moments
one of us needing the dream
more or less

Reading through these lines
I wonder if
I've used these images before

In all the confusion
it isn't easy to know

It isn't easy to know
either
when we are lost
stunned by the limits
of truth

Russell

TALK IS FOREVER

If you want to
then I will take you
to all the depths you desire
You can feed me
all that's within you
You know I can't put you down

I will step inside your dark domain
I'm the healer now I've changed my name
I will take you where there is no blame
and talk is forever

I am your punch ball
I am your downfall
I am your strange open arms
Maybe you use me
Spit on or indulge me
in all this misery rain

I will step inside your dark domain
I'm the healer now I've changed my name
I will take you where there is no blame
and talk is forever

We would not be here
if this were simple
I could just walk away
I'm in a cold room
You're in a warm room
Is there really that much that we can say?
This is hopeless
I just need someone
to share this dark side of my moon
What do you care?
You're really not there
Just another fabled design

You must need me since you turned this way
I've no answers though they're locked away
in hearts of ships that dock in no one's bay
and nothing's forever

Paul

UNTITLED

We all know him
this man
who comes in on a bad morning
or a weary afternoon
exchanging the rain and the road
and his tired feet
for the small warm dark room
three chairs
the table with its
potted plant
and the box of tissues
he no more needs

From the hostel down the road
via Leeds and Liverpool
and suchlike places
after the teachers
the social workers
and the doctors
for a cup of tea, a biscuit

his eyes slide over yours
not waiting to be seen
he would like to sleep

he sits and nods
and maunders now and then
he knows the routine

Marie

LAMBRUSCO AND A LEMON SLICE

Retreat, they called it,
Relax, she thought,
Not fraught.

Tranquil Suffolk embraced her weary self,
The promise of Spring,
Pure, pale shades lightened the horizon.
Speak in hushed tones, tread gently,
Lest a late frost kill the hope;
A sharp retort and damage done.

Tudor chimneys spiral smokeless and serene,
Twisted thoughts; what is the issue?
White or black smoke?
Still no decision.

Fragile smiles disguise fear,
Small talk masks confusion,
Tragedy and Comedy reappear,
'Whatever you're going through . . . '
Why am I here?

Retreat, they called it,
Relax, she thought
And caught
Unexpectedly some insight,
All too soon lost.

Queen Bess slept here, they said.
Slept?
Rested?
And awoke to continue the journey
In pursuit of an unknown future.

Outside, tangled weeds and twisted yew
Bore witness to four hundred years of turmoil;
And three days more.
Some tears?
Their fears
Of what may be lost,
Looking forward yet in retreat.
Re-treat, she thought,
The issues, then return to nought.

Maggie

UNSPOKEN THOUGHTS

I feel a gentle presence here
    working around the phones.
There is a quiet reasoning
    spoken in silent tones.

We sit, we wait, we speak
    and hope our voices find their way
Simply to help us listen
    to what you have to say.

And how are you tonight my friend?
I think of you, you know.
Last night I had to walk back home
through wind and rain and snow -
But oh, when I got in, my friend,
the fire had a glow . . .
I thought of you once more, my friend
and sensed your fear and woe.

And, as my comforts and my joys
    relieve me of my day,
I think of you, as I lie down -
I think of you, and pray.

Beth

6 AM

I have listened, I have bled
My soul dry feeling their pain.
Trying to understand
The hurt they feel inside.

So much pain. So many ways
To hurt another human
Being. - I don't understand! -
But the agony remains.

I am drained, weak and helpless,
I'm impotent and alone.
But my soul will fill again
Will theirs? God only knows.

Charles

DESPAIR

What is day to me?

No anticipated alarum!
My eyes and consciousness shudder
Against the light they know has come.
I want to say 'Adieu'
Long before day has begun!

A struggle to retain my isolation,
But I wake -
Resignation! Work till light is gone!
Time, through labour, is a flight to dark!

What is day to me?
A necessary journey to eternal night.

Kathy

FROZEN ICE-LOLLY

Quietly standing with a collecting tin
Knowing how a frozen ice-lolly must feel,
Two woollies were needed, this coat's too thin,
Pull icy hands under its sleeves.

Cover blue-white fingers; sense the red nose,
The smile has set in a foolish clenched grin.
The forecast was rain, not promise of snow,
Brace back to an easterly wind.

Helpers are few who will silently beg,
Wear the bright sash and not rattle the tin.
Time slowly drags past as feet turn to lead;
Invisible charity hint.

'Thanks', breaks the penance as cheering coins *clink*,
Encouragement a while longer to stay.
Ask 'why to a charity should you give?'
It could be for you some day.

Amy

IN THE INTERVIEW ROOM

Devils
Are stealing your life
You say
Sometimes your mouth opens and
Devil words come out

Tact cordons off my private disbelief
Besides
That small horned figure at your shoulder
Now smiling
Did not come in with you

Sam

WHY

Most of us die before we need
due to circumstances and the way of life that we lead.

There are a few of us who, through despair,
due to tremendous torments they can no longer bear

Whether real or imagined, trivial or great
they pass away by their own hand, through heaven or hell's gate.

There was no one to stop them, no one to intercede
no one to help them in their hour of need,
no one to help them draw back from the brink
no one to help them stop and think.

If only we were able to contact and speak to them first
would the outcome and ending be any worse.

People who have a desperate need not to stay alive
need all the time in the world to revive
It is on our time, that they hopefully thrive.

A Samaritan talks to the lonely, the confused, the old, the abused,
the tearful, the sad, the desperate, the mad.

Sometimes to help them laugh, sometimes help them cry,
sometimes help them stop asking, "Why?"

So is the job so daunting, so onerous, so difficult, so immense,
"Of course!"
That's why the vacancies are filled by ordinary people with
good old common sense.

Howard

ALIENATION

Alone, isolated, imprisoned,
surrounded by people,
by noise, by bustling business,
by happy chatter -
invisible, rejected.
The world goes on,
the sun shines,
my walls enclose me.
I feel myself a million miles removed
from all the concourse.
I tried to be part of it,
once I thought I was.
I clutched a hand that led me there -
but it was made of sand
and trickled away through my fingers.
Now it is even colder and darker where I stand.
It's not worth
the effort anymore.
There's no role here for me -
I'll watch the play
and scream inside.

Vi

WAITING

I'm waiting for the time
when the homeless get a bed,

I'm waiting for the politicians to all agree instead of arguing
and arguing with nothing at the end.

I'm waiting for peace to break out everywhere,

The things I'm waiting for above may never never come
so - I'm here waiting by the phone, a Sam volunteer.
I'm here waiting for that call to show someone we are here.

Frank

ALL I HAVE

Just an ordinary duty on a fairly drab day
But I don't suppose this caller sees it that way
His pride makes him turn away to hide his tears
His voice falters, as he hides his fears.

How can I ever understand what he's been through
My eyes have never seen life from his view
How will I with my much blessed life
Start to console this man mourning his wife.

If I wipe the lines round the eyes time has made
Can I make them lessen or fade.
If I run my hands across his damaged heart
Will it be enough to ease the smart.

Do you see the point that I'm trying to make
For the past 2 hours, I've felt no more than a fraud or a fake.
I have so little of any use, that I can give
And nothing I can think of will make you want to live.

Outside the traffic seems to hurtle by
As the sun fades into darkness in the evening sky
There's a timeless quality to the dusty gloom
That matches the mood within this room.

It's as though the rest of the world no longer exists
Oh I know it's out there just hidden in the mists
Just as I know you'll soon leave, going into the night
And I shall never know any more of your plight.

Your wife has so recently been lain to rest
And left you hurt, lonely, frightened and bereft
I mind that you are hurt, and I share your despair
I feel your anger, and truly I care.

I'm no goddess that can magic away your pain
Whatever words I use, that will remain
But here, give me your hands, put them in mine
I'll give you all I have, and that is my time.

Angela

SPYHOLE

No sound
To penetrate
The long weekend.
No knock disturbs
The empty hall.

She peers
Through the spyhole
Of the door
Municipal green.
No one.

A double ring
Threatening.
Their gazes
Lock and bulge.
The spyhole knows.

Samaritans
A disembodied
Voice. Warm.
A chain rattles
'You've come' she says.

Gillian

WHO CAN I TURN TO?

Who can I turn to? There's no-one there.
Loneliness, hopelessness, deep despair.
These feelings come, they stay all day,
I've got to make them go away.

Who can I turn to? I'm all alone,
There must be someone I can phone.
My thoughts run deep, I have no friends
I hope this loneliness soon ends

Who can I turn to? I need to talk,
Perhaps I'll try and take a walk.
The city's quiet, it's like a tomb,
Perhaps I'll go back to my room

Who can I turn to, where can I go?
There must be some place, I don't know.
Where I can go and ease the pain
And maybe feel alive again?

Who can I turn to? I don't know.
I'm all alone, I feel so low.
My faithful partner long since died,
Perhaps it's time for suicide.

Tablets swallowed, whisky too,
What else is there I can do?
Something more than sit and wait
Thinking of my coming fate.

Who'll talk to me, who'll be my friend?
Who'll help me make it to the end?
Suicide . . . the final choice!
I long to hear a friendly voice.

Who can I turn to, who can I trust?
Who will listen? Somebody must
My time is come the end is nigh.
I only want to say . . . *Goodbye*

Pick up the phone and dial out,
I hope that someone hears my shout
This cry for help, this desperate plea.
Will anybody talk to me?

Who can I turn to, who can I call?
I saw a poster on a wall,
Lonely, worried, in distress
Should I call? The answer's yes.

Tom

TOMORROW

Tomorrow, with its many ills,
its cruel demands and endless bills,
and promises it will not keep,
a golden harvest that I cannot reap.

Tomorrow, I'll sail on tranquil seas,
where mind and soul will be at ease,
Or with God's heavenly angels soar,
to where he's waiting at the door.

Tomorrow, from this earth I leave,
I wear my heart upon my sleeve,
like the fruitful dahlia seed,
in a bed of roses, is but a weed.

Tomorrow, my spirit will be free,
Those years of torment end for me,
Peace at last I will have found,
as they lay my body in the ground.

Tomorrow, my family will shed a tear,
Friends will come from far and near,
and ask the question, why O' why,
So happy, so good, so young to die.

Tom

FEELINGS

Feelings of suicide, feelings of despair,
Feeling sad and lonely,
Why won't someone care?

Feeling of rejection and of pure defeat,
At times like this it's certain,
Death it would be sweet.

Feeling paranoiac, life's got it in for you.
When you look into the future,
Doom and gloom shine through.

Feeling of desertion, no way can you win,
For as long as you remember,
To be happy was a sin.

Feeling of being dirty, of being badly used,
When your flesh is sore and aching,
And your spirit has been bruised.

Feeling in deep water, so far into debt,
The faster that you paddle,
The deeper in you get.

Feeling so unlucky, in life you are a loser,
Everyone you counted on,
Seems to have been a user.

Feeling you're not normal, your desires are not au fait,
You don't fit in with anyone,
Can't face another day.

Feelings that take over, violence and crime,
You've had eight lives already,
Only cats get nine.

Feelings you don't want to share, with anyone at all,
You'd rather walk alone the plank,
Trust comes before a fall.

Feeling that you're pregnant, what are you to do?
It was just a one night stander,
And he's not the man for you.

Feeling that your family take you for a ride,
You have no right to anything,
Your needs they sweep aside.

No matter what your problem is,
We're always here for you,
No matter what the time is,
Dial and you get through.

We want to share your feelings,
To lend a listening ear,
To us you are important,
That's why we are here

You may remain anonymous,
Your name we won't pursue,
The only thing that matters,
Is no-one else but you.

You don't even have to talk to us,
Until you want to do,
We've got time and loads of patience,
We'll wait around for you.

We don't close down on Sundays,
And our days don't have an end,
We're here at your disposal,
Anytime you need a friend.

We never sit in judgement
Or push our point of view,
The only thing that matters,
Is pure and simply - *You.*

Your calls are confidential,
Your secrets we won't share,
We're only here to listen,
And let you know we care.

Feelings are important,
So when you're in despair,
Get in touch with a Samaritan,
You'll find - we're always there!

Freda Lightfoot

SOMEONE STRANGE

One day she lost her love.
It drained away,
the last of it,
under the sick sun
one arid coming home
when she picked up
from the hard hot path
the soft child,
his cries and whimpers.
And the mother came,
brimful blame and sharp,
said to her child,
if you will run off and fall
you get strange people.
That was when she lost
the last of her love,
the love
for the strange woman,
herself,
and tear sightless stepped
off the curb
into white silence.

Jenny

LISTENING

The phone is ringing! Hello, can I help?
Oh, I do hope so, says a voice.
It's my husband, you see, I've thrown him out
But really I had no choice.
He's always hitting me and the kids
Especially when he's had a drink
So I told him to go, which he readily did,
Now I feel as if I'm on the brink.
When he's had a drink he's disgusting,
He hits me and the kids all he can,
But when he's sober he's lovely,
And damn it, I still love the man.
In spite of his drinking and gambling,
And the women he's had on the side,
I love him more now than I did on the day
I walked down the aisle as a bride!
We've never had any money,
He spends it on horses and beer.
He's got a good job, but he'll lose it,
If he doesn't alter his ways, never fear!
I won't be dramatic or stupid,
That would leave the kids on their own.
I just needed to talk and let it all out,
That's why I picked up the phone.
But what will I do now, without him?
Do you think p'raps he'll come back to me?
Well thanks very much just for listening,
I'll go now, the kids are home for their tea
How do you tackle a problem like this?
Many times I can feel the tears glisten,
But they usually know we can't do anything
They just want someone there who will *listen!*

Gillian

THE LISTENERS

Who are they, this nameless throng,
Who judge not what is right or wrong
Listening patiently night and day
Doing their best come what may
To help with problems, big and small
No matter who or why they call?

Depressed, lonely, just can't cope,
Wanting to be given hope.
Sometimes it's a love affair
One of them has ceased to care,
But the tragic ones are those who cry,
Don't let me live, I want to die.

So forgetting one's own fears,
And often holding back the tears,
I'm here, I care, don't hang up please,
Striving to comfort, to ease
The pain they feel, to soothe their sorrow
Though it may be there tomorrow.

Of all ages from all places,
Of no account their names or faces,
Day and night they are there,
Hold on, I'm listening, I care.

Sheila Smith

MY SON

'Samaritans, can I help you?'
That's what I said.
The one she had loved, had gone away.
'He was so beautiful' she said.
Beautiful, a face like an angel.
A smile that beamed love.
He had written her a letter
Begging her forgiveness, assuring her, his love.
She read it so poetic.
My tears I could not stop.
I started to feel, her great sense of loss.
He was only nineteen.
Still only a child.
She had given him life,
and had watched him grow.
Her beautiful son, had wanted to go.
Had taken his life, his heart so low.
She thanked me for listening,
and put down the phone.
My job I had done,
and I had given her what?
A few minutes of time, nothing more nothing less.
I remember a great sense of uselessness.
My duty was over,
Time to go home.
Back to my family, I'm never alone.
I opened the door, there was his small face.
A smile like an Angel, and the warmest embrace.

Sarah

I'M SORRY TO BE A BURDEN

I'm sorry to be a burden
I'm sorry to waste your day
I don't seem to know, now that I've rung
Just what I wanted to say . . .
I need to get things straight in my mind
If it's alright I'll talk anyway
Everything seems to be falling apart
My mind's going round and around
But if you can just go on listening to me
It'll help get my feet on the ground.
The life that I live is in turmoil
And all that was good is destroyed
I don't even think I can start again
When there's nothing much left I enjoyed
The person who means the world to me
Is gone now and I'm all alone
I can't bear the loneliness, just cannot see
What the point is in carrying on . . .
It's good of you to listen to me
Though others are greater in need
But you make me feel it's important
And maybe there's reason to grieve
And what's going on inside my head
Seems to make some kind of a sense
It doesn't stop hurting, or the pain
But now I don't feel quite so tense
And I know there's somebody listening to me
Who cares, so if you don't mind
I think I might ring you again some time
When things get too much to bear.

Thank you so much for listening to me
And for sharing in my despair
I think I can try now to get some sleep
And then I might get some fresh air
As long as I know I can call again
And there's somebody there all the time
I think I'll be able to cope with the pain
All alone at the end of the line.

Angela

SECRETS

Their secrets are locked in the telephone booth
Exploring the pain like a tongue in a tooth.
Does the lady in black wish to die
Or just try - to re-route her life?

And what of the wife of the man about town?
Still loving him dearly - she's some kind of clown?
But his passion still drubs at her ego, her self
As she's left on the shelf of his own self-esteem

His tame Kitchen Queen.

His Bit-On-The-Side, on her given nights
Puts her lust to the fore.
And dispensing fidelity wishes for more of him,
Wanting his kitchen, usurping his Queen,
But lonely sits ringing in that other scene
When she isn't the one, the public expression
of marital bliss, of family life,
But hid in a closet and let out at night.

And so playing the game of love, dare or truth,
They whisper their minds in the telephone booth.

Vernice Bacon-Darnley

SAM'S SONG

I walked the paths of loneliness
And wondered could it be
That maybe I should end it
And be trouble free

But then life is not easy
It can deal some tough blows
The highways and byways
Are very narrow roads

One day when I sat thinking
What being a Sam could be
It didn't seem easy
But maybe it's for me

Not some one who is judging
Or telling you what to do
But some one who's listening
Because they've been there too

So somewhere in my darkness
There has been a voice for me
And that's the only reason
I am sitting here you see

I really am quite human
And know turmoil too
Life being what it is today
I can empathise with you

It is not in education
Or the knowledge I can share
It is just the simple listening
And the time that I can spare

So being a good Samaritan
Is simply being me
And being there and caring
For someone else, not me.

Elizabeth

A SAMARITAN DUTY

Just going on duty
Wondering what it will bring
Having sat down the telephone rings
A lady's been battered
A young girl's been raped
There's a man wants the number
Of the nearest AA
Someone rings and just wants to cry
Silent callers who try and try
People on drugs who want to come off
Someone's taken tablets and wants to die
Regular callers who say we're their friends
An old man grieves over the death of his wife
A transvestite coming to terms with his life
A boy's left home with nowhere to go
A man threatens to cut his wrists
because he's feeling so low
A schoolgirl's getting bullied
because she is gay
Someone rings to say thanks for today
As my duty comes to an end
I give thanks for support of colleagues and friends
Always glad I was there
To give comfort listen and to care.

Marion

SOMEONE TO TALK TO

I just want someone to talk to
Someone to listen to me
There's no light at the end of the tunnel
Please put an arm around me.

Everyone else is so busy
All wrapped up with their future plans
I can't burden the kids with my problems
and friends may not understand.

Perhaps they'd be better without me
I have thoughts about ending it all
Then I saw your name on a poster
and decided to give you a call.

I just want someone to talk to
Someone to listen to me
Someone to unload to
Samaritan please put your arms around me.

Pat

THE VISITOR

I saw him by the doorway
shoulders huddled tight against the inner storm
Decades of pain painted upon his face
Loneliness and rejection written in his gait
Hesitantly deciding to approach us
And I wondered - I wondered would listening be enough?

I saw him walk tall through the doorway
Inner strength revisited
Peace flitting across his craggy face
And I stood in awe - I stood in awe at the magic of
this encounter.

Ann

THE PRISONER

Dressed in khaki shorts, shirt and unlaced pumps
the pris'ner from the strip cell shuffles in
And with downcast eyes in a chair he slumps.
Freedom gone. Sorrow and despair for him.

Two visiting Sams prepared to listen.
A wayward lonely youth stepped out of line
Apprehensive and banged up in prison
Despairingly he thinks, and bides his time.

At last Bill talks of burglary and drugs.
Of booze bereavement violence and death
Black days and blacker nights, but he just shrugs.
Brooding thoughts like a web strangle his breath.

No internal flame lights the way ahead.
No flame burns off the black web of sorrow.
The outlook's bad; He might as well be dead.
Sad Bill will he make it till tomorrow?

Friendless and forlorn; No one cares a damn.
But is there maybe a flickering smile?
Perhaps a latent dormant spark to fan
As Bill talks about his six month old child.

Down claustrophobic echoing corridors we retreat,
Through clanging iron gates to freedom in the street,
Exchanging thoughts of frustration helplessness and concern
To the Centre two Samaritans return.

Two visiting Sams who tried to listen.
Bill meanwhile sorts out his thoughts in prison.

Back at the Centre the phone is ringing.
It's Bill from prison. 'Thanks Sams for caring'

Bill

SAMARITANS

I joined the Samaritans recently
I thought it a noble thing to do
To help people with their problems
And hopefully see them through

I am finding it absorbing
And think my time is well invested
And I hope to help more people
By showing I am interested

I am learning slowly
How to help people that are depressed
Although I am not qualified yet
With the leaders I am impressed

Their acting is impressive
It really makes you think
Just how desperate people get
And how low they feel they sink

These people need our help
We may be their last hope
With gentle talk and coaxing
We may convince then they can cope

I hope we help most people
It is really quite a test
I know it is not going to be easy
But I am going to try my best

June

THE CALLER

Alone, the dial gazes at me
The love ended, where did I fail?
The silence, no future can I see
Can a voice help as at fate I rail.
Please, please, listen to my hurt, my guilt
My feelings I needs must summon
Listen, listen, frenzied words to the hilt.
My lonely despair, is it common
The future so bleak, where can I hide
What point the past to cherish?
Now unveiled the prescience of suicide
Unless convinced 'tis better not to perish.
Desperate emotions, disorder is rife
Where there's no hope can there be life?

Douglas

THE LOSS OF A LOVED ONE

A death means pain
You think you will never be the same again
You will
Everything you find reminds you of your loss
Then the tears flow
One feels so low
A short time has passed
The pain gently eases
We learn to live again
Anything we find reminds how happy we were
We can laugh and remember the things we did
At last our grief is much lighter
Our future is much brighter
Because we have learned to live again.

Sally

UNTITLED

I love breakfast on Saturdays,
Cheerful crockery and the table properly laid;
My home-made marmalade and the smell of toast
And we, together, weekending - sharing the local paper.
I scan the pages, council meeting, jumble sales
And letters of protest against the new bypass.

Then 'Father of Three Found Dead'
I hear again his voice in the night,
Hopeless and fearful, close to my ear -
The loss of his job, the mounting debts,
Another baby due quite soon,
And now the house to go as well.
He *must* find the courage to tell his wife.
But he couldn't!

Now I taste a tiny morsel of his despair,
For I had striven to instil a spark of hope
And I had failed!

Into my thoughts another voice is breaking
'Are you listening love - do you want more coffee?'
How I wish I could claim the comfort of his arms.

. . .

Nerves a-jangle, ill tempered, cold,
The check out queue seemed endless;
The rain persistent, and the bus was
Overcrowded and late, late, late.

Arriving, barely time to remove my coat
And the telephone rings.

Such loneliness, isolated and bereft,
I feel the blackness of her life.
We talk about the death of her husband
And the burdens of old age.
Then 'You've brought light into my day!'
And no amount of sunshine, empty shops
And buses running on time
Could compete with this moment.

Gill

THE QUESTION OF HOPE

Why am I here? Do I help?
Do I sound caring? I can only try;
there are no magic answers, just a listening ear,
a stranger to trust, a shoulder on which to cry.

Wrong numbers, silence, sexual abuse,
ear bending complaints, I'm rarely of use;
and yet to these callers I must believe I help,
or just submit and join them
in this world ailing with social disease;
full of confused frightened people who believe
they must complete what others have begun,
to finish their life and this world as one.

Do I care enough outside the Samaritans?
can I care too much and risk changing places;
A Samaritan's world is frustratingly hollow.
For as doubts turn to thoughts of failure
a few words, 'thank you, you've helped me'
a saving call, gives me hope.
And hope is all I can give to anyone,
everyone who really wants to live.

Gloster White

SHAKING

I never expected the shaking.
'I've taken some tablets. I don't want help,
Just someone to talk to as I die.'

I didn't shake in the rôle-play,
Thought I'd handled it quite well,
Kept my cool, talked things through,
The tutor had even agreed, eventually, that I could call an ambulance.

But this was different
A mug of coffee cooling, slowly, by the log book,
My first sip had won over the third ring of the phone,
It was still hot and strong in my mouth when

'I've taken some tablets. I don't want help,
Just someone to talk to as I die.'

And I shook.

My mind was in rôle-play, calm, collected,
We spoke of her feelings, what she'd actually taken,
What had brought her to this, and, again,
'Can we call an ambulance?'

But my body was in real life,
The real life of someone that was soon to be lost,
Uncontrollable shaking that threatened my voice,
Threatened my composure, threatened my certainty.

We spoke some more, she sounded as calm as I,
This time she would do it, this time there would be no help,
There was no point to life, now he was gone,
And perhaps she'd call later, when the pills took more effect.

But by that time, I'd be away, my duty done,
And she'd be refusing help from another volunteer.
They made me a fresh cup of coffee, said I'd done good,
The Leader was quiet and sympathetic when I 'phoned.

In my last hour there weren't any more calls,
And the knot in my stomach slowly melted away,
But down in the carpark, as I unlocked my car,
The keys shook in my hand.

Michael

I AM A SAMARITAN

I do not judge
I accept you as you are
I may not always agree
These feelings I keep only for me
We meet as equals
For I am a Samaritan.

I have made a commitment
To which I'll stand true
Confidentiality anonymity
To me are not new
We are off one
For I am a Samaritan

I don't claim to solve problems
When the answers lie within
You need to talk
Your choice when to begin
Feel free to be with me
For I am a Samaritan

So you ask the question
You ask why I'm here
The answer is simple
No suspicion or fear
There's no monetary gain or professional flair
The reason I'm a Samaritan
Is because I care.

Caroline

SUICIDE NOTE

Should anybody miss me
Tell them
'She drowned in the ocean of her own tears
Shed day after day in the darkness of a lonely bedroom.
One night the salty waves just closed over her head.'

Should anybody ask you
Tell them
'She sank in the quagmire of her own despondency.
Several times she dragged herself back on to dry land
But the straws she clutched at were all false hopes.'

Should anybody wonder
Tell them
'She was poisoned by the dregs of her own bitterness.
It wasn't a quick death because it was administered in small doses
But it must have accumulated in a vital organ.'

Should there be any questions
Tell them
'She was asphyxiated by the silence of her own solitude.
Some people have been killed by the noise of a jet engine
But she died because no one ever said the words she needed to hear.'

Should there be any queries
Tell them
'She was crushed by the weight of her own responsibilities.
Doing a full day's work in a job that brought little reward
And then coming home to a dirty house and four fatherless children.'

If you are ever challenged
Tell them
'She died of starvation due to a deficiency
Of essential affection and moral support in her emotional diet.
Actually she had suffered malnutrition of this kind for several years.'

Should anybody really miss me
Never admit the truth
'She was murdered.'

Louise

OUT OF THIS

Out of this muddle -
this interminable tangle
of uncertain days
I call you.

Out of nights ghosted
by insidious whispers
of past transgressions
I call you.

Out of this chaos -
my token resolutions
broken again and again
I call you.

But when I see
black buds break through
on battered branches
I hear you.

As aconites rise
brave above last drifts
of greying snow
I hear you.

And slowly
I begin to know
a personal resurrection.

Margaret Connor

03.37

Your tears of shame
Your tears of sorrow
Your tears of those
maybe might of tomorrows
You hurt
You cry
You ache
You sigh
Been told
Be brave
Never mind
Soon fade
Now scream
and shout
and swear
be speechless
rant
and
rave
you are
afraid
We won't judge
won't advise
We will listen
won't decide
Like us
or loathe us
Love us
and leave us
We will listen
without derision
Whatever your dark
personal prison.

Peter

TELEPHONE

I sit and wait.
This instrument and coil of wire become a fancied threat
and I begin to tire with waiting and anxiety.

When that bell rings how can I enter someone's hell
and stay composed? I cannot tell, when that bell rings,
if I can look into a cold well of despair
and hang on for a while. Will a twisting pain
entrap me like a snare? Will all about me gel
when that bell rings and my heart turn to stone?
I feel so lone.

Doubting for a while, not sure, I study the sunlit
patterns on the floor; and then my eyes turn back
to that black instrument - it now seems gentler than before.

If I could stop the pounding of my heart and this anxiety cease
some good at last may come - perhaps some peace.
So let there be an end to this destructive strife
and let my hand hold firm this link with life.
At least to this faint hope I'll cling.
I'll now sit here and wait - wait for this phone to ring.

Gordon

UNTITLED

Minor courage,
A pause of breath,
A flicker of nerve endings
As the phone drills.

Grown fearless, we would meddle.

Catherine Whalen

GIVE ME HOPE SAMARITAN

I'm tired Samaritan
so tired of being scared.
I've contemplated suicide
but I don't want to die.
It's easier to drown,
down in my own despair.

I'm scared Samaritan
so scared of being tired.
I've tried to leave
but I've nowhere to go.
It's easier to stay,
pretend and carry on.

You ask me to take it slowly,
          talk about it, make it real.
Stretch your arms out calm Samaritan
          come on a journey, make me feel.

Can you hear my swirling thoughts?
Feel my anger, my hurt, my pain.
Can you hear my anguish calling?
This is where I come to time and time again.

          I'm crying Samaritan
          crying out to you.
          I've tried to share my thoughts
          but all too often I'm alone.
Listen to me Samaritan
          And give me hope.

Paula

CALLER AND SAM

Shy at first,
cursed
By feelings
overun
With emotions
flowing
Words staggering,
out pouring
fear and anger roaring -
through tears leaving nothing
no hope
through eyes seeing nothing
no joy
Their very soul in pain
What can callers' gain?
Quiet confidence
listening Empathetic calm
speaking

Annie Corsie

CRIES FOR HELP

Please, please help me, help me, please, please help me
I'm so alone, so very alone, my heart aches.
Please, please help me, help me, please, please help me.

Nobody cares, nobody wants to know about my troubles,
I'm desperate, nobody cares.
Please, please help me, help me, please, please help me.

I can't think straight, I'm confused, my life is
no longer worth living.
Please, please help me, help me, please, please help me.

I'm afraid, I'm scared, I'm frightened of death,
I don't know what will become of me?
Please, please help me, help me, please, please help me.

The loss is so, so painful, I can't describe the pain,
I don't want to carry on, there's nothing left. I want
to die, there's nothing to live for now, nothing.
Please, please help me, help me, please, please help me.

I can't tell you how guilty I feel, I can't bear the
thoughts any longer, I want to end it all.
Please, please help me, help me, please, please help me.

I feel useless, I'm worthless, I am utterly, utterly miserable.
I just want the pain to go away. I've cried all night.
Please, please help me, help me, please, please help me.

Nobody understands how I feel, it's so unfair, this
body doesn't belong to me. Why have I had to suffer
all my life, why, why?
Please, please help me, help me, please, please help me.

It's the hurt I feel so deeply hurt, I just can't
understand how one person could be so hurtful to
another, not somebody they're supposed to love.
The pain won't go away, why won't it go away?
Please, please help me, help me, please, please help me.

I've just had enough, I can't cope any longer, I've
lost everything, my business, my wife, my family.
Everything is finished, I've just had enough, I want to die.
Please, please help me, help me, please, please help me.

I don't understand, I can't understand why little children
have to suffer. I've had my life, why couldn't it be me. I
feel so angry, so very angry.
Please, please help me, help me, please, please help me.

This is the Samaritans - can I help you?

Jim 427

BATTERED WIVES

Battered rocks
Relentless waves
Broken outlines
Crevices forming
Tear channels
Stalwart.

Barnacles clinging to breasts
Cannot leave
Heavy hearts of stone
Deep rooted
Love.

High tide
Suppressive peace
Barnacles plucked
Caressing sorrow
Garlands of brown sea weed
Sighing.

Rose 1

HOW I BECAME A SAMARITAN VOLUNTEER

Strange how an event
Can change the course of one's life -
And send one down a road
Less travelled - perhaps!

A past pupil unexpectedly paid me a visit -
Some years ago
A lovely 18 year old brown eyed beauty
My work space was rather cramped
So I invited her to my bedroom - to talk.

On opening the door - she simply
Stared and stared
I stood aghast - wondering!

She was starring at the telephone
On my locker
Then she threw her arms around my neck and said
'If only I had known that you had a telephone
I wouldn't have taken an overdose to kill myself.'

I felt shocked, but stayed calm
We sat on the bed and she sobbed out the whole story -
Poor Leaving Cert., no job, dole,
Poor flat - shattered relationship
I listened and listened.

We sat there for 3 hours
She came to visit me for some weeks
And all is well with her now.

This event caused me to think of joining the Samaritans
I applied and was thrilled to be accepted
At first I found the Snap Calls frustrating
And often thought 'Is my voice too rough,
Not gentle enough, or not having the right tone.'

But, of course, later I realised
That we can never tell
How many times a Caller takes up the phone before they have the courage to talk.

Suicidal calls I was afraid of at first
Listening in the silence of the night
To complete despair, loneliness and brokeness
And perhaps the sound of a box of tablets being shaken around
Reminding you of their plan.

Listening to and trying to explore feelings
And assuring them that you stay with them all the time -
I found a great help.

Perhaps in a way, too, I found it hard
Not to have further contacts with the Suicidal
as I would have loved to
This wouldn't be within the ethos of the Samaritans
So I learned to *let go*

As well as helping others
We become learners ourselves
In the different skills of dealing with another's pain
And also learning how we react ourselves in different situations.

I love my work with the Samaritans
I have met such wonderful people -
So caring, understanding and helpful -
Also so encouraging.

I find great fulfilment in my work here
So I am glad that a past event
Led me to where I am now.

A quote won't be out of order here:
'Life needs gentle and delicate Hands -
hands that know the right water for life
Just the right degree of light
At the right time
Or else, no life, no flower, no fruit, no hope.'

Sea Breezes

THE SAMARITAN

Listening on the phone with a sympathetic ear
All the troubles pour out between you and me
Releasing their troubles and secret fears
Sometimes a hopeless case is all can see
People in such gloom and so full of despair
Talking away then slamming down the phone
It might all be money or even an affair
Or worries at work that they just take home
The Samaritan is always there each day or night
Putting their problems to the back of the mind
Listening to the anger or even sheer spite
Trying to be helpful, discreet and so kind
Children are the ones that get to your heart
Why should they worry, instead of to play
Perhaps it's the parents who are going to part
The traumatic world it's the sign of today
If Samaritans can help to release the stress
To see into your life and talk things through
It's a job well done and they give their best
So if you have a crisis they are there for you

Tony A Slater

IS ANYBODY THERE?

People talk above me and try to give me their advice.
No one listens to what I have to say.
They can hide within their cosy world,
They know that they can turn and walk away.

I'm cold, I'm frightened and I'm all alone,
Please don't shut the door and leave me here.
Please don't turn your back and walk away.
Don't leave me in this hopeless world of fear.

Does anybody care, is anybody there?

Robert Montgomery

MIRROR

Darkness strikes us all.
Deep in every black hole lies a purpose.
Opening up, a place is found under the racing mind,
Beneath the sea of solitude
That allows some peace.

Blank despair beckons.
A seed of knowing deep in our being
Shows the invisible threads connecting us all.

The listener is a mirror,
The caller is a candle.
The mirror reflects the candle light
To glimpse these threads on the darkest journey.

Peter

DEEP DESPAIR

Life is sometimes boring
it can also be lonely too,
friends! there isn't many
so what am I to do.

I could talk to family
but they just shrug and stare,
they laugh when your back is turned
they just don't seem to care.

Why is it when I'm happy
something comes and knocks me down,
every one around me is smiling
all I seem to do is frown.

So who can I contact,
who can I call,
there doesn't seem anybody
Nobody at all.

I feel so alone now
unhappy and depressed,
I say to myself, 'be happy'
I really try my best.

Then one day something happened
to change my outlook on life,
the answer was written on a leaflet saw an end to my strife.

The number was for the Samaritans
So I rang and they spoke to me,
I've found someone to listen
And let my problems go free.

I now know there's someone to listen
They'll listen and hear my plea.
Not judge me on my colour
But to treat me individually.

So I've found someone to talk to
Someone my problems to share,
Thank God, there's someone to contact
When I'm in deep despair.

Teresa Webster

IDENTITY

I'm not the person I'm supposed to be.
You do not know me, so for once I'm real.
Help me reveal my true identity.

I have a major problem being me.
God alone knows how I'm meant to feel.
I'm not the person I'm supposed to be.

I'm really someone different, you see.
I cannot share my inner life at all.
Help me reveal my true identity.

If only I could change reality,
or could ignore the mirror on the wall.
I'm not the person I'm supposed to be.

I've always fantasised I could be free,
but find myself alone inside a shell.
Help me reveal my true identity.

Please listen to the things I have to say,
the secrets I have no-one else to tell.
Help me reveal my true identity.
I'm not the person I'm supposed to be.

Sheila

ABUSE - THE END OF THE INNOCENCE

From a semi-conscious state I am suddenly
aware that I am not at home
after a second or two, my initial panic subsides,
I sit up quickly, desperately trying to come to my senses.

A child's voice cuts through the stillness of the night,
arousing within me a series of profound emotions . . .
. . . until the tears well and fall

'I feel so guilty . . . why don't I stop him? . . .
I think he loves me . . . I know he does . . .
He doesn't mean to hurt me . . . are you there?
Tell me what to do . . . Oh God help me . . .
. . . please

I put down the receiver and sit up,
very much awake,
A passing car on the cobbles breaks the silence
and then there is nothing.
Nothing but the darkness, the intense feeling of
disgust for my sex, the overwhelming awareness
of my inability to do a thing to help this child
. . . This child who only seconds sooner had
implored me . . . begged me to help her

There is nothing . . . nothing but the images
in my mind

Jack

LONG TERM CALLER

Again he's on the phone
sobbing and alone.

I listen to him weeping
his sorrows through me seeping.

The desperate ache won't go away,
it's just another lonely day.

Emptiness is in his voice is in my ear,
a week, a month, a year

Again I try to visualise
the hurt I hear fall from his eyes.

Sadness on my finger tips,
lonely on his lips.

The hurt slips through.

In his despairing
is he listening to my caring?

So real the cry:
he wants to die.

There's no point, I can't go on!
He'll call tomorrow. Hope I'm not wrong.

Caroline

LOVE CONQUERS

What can I do?
Where can I go?
Blackness entombs my heart, I have lost my footing on this planet,
Lord God, everything has gone awry.
My best friends have absconded
When my need was the greatest.

A voice within whispers:
'I'll tell you what to do -
End it all; it's the only way.'
Yes, that's an answer of a kind.
or is it?
Something deep within me struggles
            to be heard:
'Life is the Creator's gift
Given once and only once.'
And so I pause.
The telephone is near,
I have dialled before.
The numbers I have off my heart.
But who is at the other end?
You've guessed it right
They're known as the Samaritans,
A soft soothing musical voice
answers -
'Can I help?'
Ah this is graced relief.
I pour out my woes, my troubles,
            my frustrations.
My 'friend' just listens.
But it's listening charged with love.
And I feel confident, comforted, consoled.
Inner healing has begun.
There's no preaching, no intimidation,
Only care and deep concern.
Few questions are asked;
But I feel loved and valued

I'm seen not as I am
But as I might become,
When love will conquer fear.
My 'friend' has time for one
And so I can relax and trust.

Slowly I am pulled back from the brink,
Rescued,
I am valued again,
Life *is* worth living
Even if experiences can crush.

Thanks dear listener for
            your time, your patience.
I am changed, changed utterly
The blackness is suffused with light.
And if ever at a future date,
I lose my way again
And fall into the abyss,
I know there's someone
Out there who *cares*.

So thanks for being there,
Thanks for your time, your deep concern.
Above all thank you for the saving power of *love*

Marie 3

A PAPER DEATH

'A young woman hanged herself
hours after discovering that
her A-level results were not
as good as she had hoped.'

The Times - 20th August 1994

Far worse things to die for
Than an A Level exam grade
So you took the hard way out
And death the price you paid

Congratulations, Charlotte
For you made the front page
For all the wrong reasons
At just twenty years of age

And whatever made you do it
It was such a useless waste
Though it was your decision
A decision taken in haste?

Now the grief and pain begins
To see afterwards what's left
But Charlotte now has nothing
For she died a paper death.

Justin

THE CALLER

The phone rings
And I answer,
You are there
And you whisper
'I am lonely'
There is silence
And then you say
'It is so hard to talk'
I know it has been difficult
For you to make this call,
I try to tell you
'It is alright
Take your time
I will wait
I care'
You share your feelings with me
You share the most important thing
You have to share
You share yourself,
I appreciate that great privilege.
I know I cannot wave a magic wand
And take away your pain
But I can listen
I can accept you
And most of all
I will not judge you,
And I hope that when you choose
To end this call
you will feel
A little more cared for
That you are, after all
A very special person.

Gretta 1

A SIMPLE SAM

So many times I've wondered how
Such luck has come to me.
I'm just a plain old working mum
With no special talents, see.

And so about three years ago
The 'ad' appeared once more
I'd thought of being a volunteer
But been too busy before.

My local branch accepted me
I went for training each week
I learnt so much in little time
To listen rather than speak.

And then my duties started
I shook from bone to bone
Who'd have thought I'd be so scared
To just pick up the phone!

Really I should have known all along
But never gave it a thought
The volunteers had become my friends
They gave me strength and support.

If I have helped in any way
I can't have asked for more
You never know who's on the phone
Or knocking at the door.

The callers who are in distress
Their problems may be vast
The suicidal and depressed
Found courage to speak at last.

And now we've become 'Friends of the Sams'
Myself and family too
The money is needed for many things
But raised by just a few.

Now galas, auctions, quizzes too
The hard work's just begun
But who'd think raising money
Could ever be such fun.

So my life is now much richer
With the Sams I'm never alone
I hope these words have touched a chord
Excuse me - that's the phone!

Brenda

CAN I HELP?

Can you help?
Probably not an awful lot.
I can't make your heartache or hurting stop.

So why are you there?
Because I care,
And I hope you'll tell me how you feel.

You don't know what it's like for me!
Maybe you can let me through?
Through to your darkness -
Is there room there for two?

Room? There's plenty of room.
It's like a big black hole, all around me.
Please, can I come in?
Maybe together we can find a key.

Clare

RINGING THE SAMARITANS

Although I call, I know you can't help me,
it's all gone wrong and I am on my own.
There's no hope left, I'm sure you will agree.

Friends warn me I've grown bitter, but I see
they have each other while I sleep alone.
Although I call, I know you can't help me.

My sap fails, I am dying like a tree
riddled with worm, half blasted, overgrown.
There's no hope left. I'm sure you will agree

I'm quite poetic, but I'm forty-three,
invisible to men now youth has flown
although I call. I know you can't help me

even to pray. I cannot bend the knee:
he lets the loveless reap what they have sown.
There's no hope left, I'm sure you will agree.

The Doctor gives me pills. No remedy.
I've got the empty bottle by the phone.
Although I call, I know you can't help me:
there's no hope left, I've forced you to agree.

Sue

UNTITLED

Cry sleeps around room, around phone,
Moth life the voices of the ones
The sad ones, the bad ones,
The ones we do not want,
Who is to listen then?

Thoughts of leaving giving them a thrill
Life sticks in their throats, a powdery pill
they scream, they dream,
Unable to speak,
Who is to listen then?

Guilt and remorse they wrap in a note,
Leaving makes s close in life so remote,
They are abused, angry,
Talking lonely sex,
Who is to listen then?

Suspend them on a wire that cannot hold,
My life seductive trying to enfold,
I am tired, I am lonely,
Finally at a loss
You let go the line.

Kim Foster

NO ONE'S THERE

'Thc Samaritans,
can I help you?'
I don't know
Can you?

I'm alone you see
where no-one knows
how I feel.
They're all too busy
in their own Worlds.

My World is black
from the inside out.
And life is black
from too much doubt.
My heart is empty
from too much fear.
And life is empty
from no-one near.
The pain I bear is
so very heavy.
I can't carry on
if life's like this.
All I want
is quiet bliss.
Confusion rules the day
And no,
it's not okay.
Night used to be
the time I felt
most lonely.
But now day
is darker still.
The pain I bear is
so very heavy.
Your advert asks
'Lonely, depressed?'

To which I answer -
Yes!
No-one listens anymore.
But then,
I don't always talk anymore
except inside my head
where it's safe,
but scary.
Can you understand?
Can you help?
Can you fix my life?
It's the pain,
inside.
I feel
like I'm drowning,
in a life of people.
And no-one's there
For me.

Martin

IMAGINARY CONVERSATION (THE OTHER END)

I am so tired (so tired)
- Of listening to you 'listening' to me
  Why don't you just wrap up and let me talk.
  That's what I rang for!

I am so quiet (so quiet)
- And now you're getting talkative
  Because you think I don't want to speak:
  If truth be told, I'm just dying to, but . . .

I am so angry (so angry)
- At you for being there, while I have to be
  Here, in this situation.

I am so down (so down)
- And all you can do is be your nice,
  Happy, jolly self and not realise my down-ness.

Here I am again:
I am so tired (so tired)
- Of life
            goodbye

Julian

THE KING OF SPAIN

He wears a dark fedora
to guard against the rain
and gently holds a secret:
he should be King of Spain.
For somewhere on the bloodline,
a lax duenna strayed
and passion flared in old Madrid
and from it he was made.

A cup of tea he nurses
and lisps his old refrain.
There's someone gently listening;
They'll hear it all again.
For if you're truly regal
the world is so unjust,
there's jibes and jokes and ridicule
and no-one you can trust.

And when the hour's over
back to his room he goes
to gently face reality,
or so the record shows,
that when your mother beat you,
you never knew your dad,
You gently, deftly, slip away
where things are not so bad.

R E Anthony

LISTEN

Listen to the ring that calls for help
    That penetrates our ordered lives
    And makes hearts jump in expectation
    Of what awaits the ready ear.

Listen to the tension in the silence
    That speaks so loud of shame or hurt or fear
    But stumbles seeking one prepared to share
    Those inner tears, that sense of loss so real.

Listen to the words sounding so wooden
    That introduce a story grim and sad
    As if no one could ever understand
    That world so crazy and distorted.

Listen to those feelings gushing forth
    The floodgates opened, no-one now can stop
    The pouring out of years of pent-up pain
    Until exhaustion stills the throbbing frame.

Listen to the threats to life itself
    The anger or resentment deep within
    That forces minds to think the worst
    About one's worth in other people's eyes.

Listen to the sounds of words less tense
    That recognise an understanding ear
    Feeling the strength of new support
    Even with no certain goal to gain.

Listen to the plans for future days
    Suggesting hope at last re-kindled
    And with possibilities of further talk
    To work at life with those who care.

Listen to the anxious thoughts and minds
Of both the sender and recipient of words
For who can bear the burden of the story
And stay untouched by such despair.

Brian

WHO?

The people who care
Are those people who share
In the problems of others unknown.
They will listen all night
To anyone's plight,
Disregarding the views of their own.

Control of their feeling
In all of their dealings
With suicide, death and despair,
May be hard to contain
But their spirits maintained,
As back up is constantly there.

They give up their leisure
In hours they don't measure
Assigned to a red telephone.
With an ever cocked ear
To rape, torment and fear,
Just to say 'You are never alone'.

So let us discover
Those who act like a mother
On duty the full clock each day.
It's to them others turn
When life's path starts to spurn
They're simply called 'Sams' (without pay).

Ann

WE'RE HERE FOR YOU

I'm here for you, I hear your voice,
I'll listen to you cry.
We'll feel your pain together,
When you say you want to die.

You try to tell your story
And all you think you lack.
There's no point looking forward,
It's too painful looking back.

You tell your tale of sorrow.
You say there's no one there,
Who'll listen to your anguish
And show you that they care.

But, I'm here for you, I hear your voice,
I'll listen to you cry.
We'll feel your pain together,
When you say you want to die.

You say you've taken tablets,
Maybe fifty, could be more,
You drowned them with some whisky
And you've locked your bedroom door.

There's more tablets on the table,
Just in case it's not enough.
You don't want to wake tomorrow
Just feeling bad and looking rough.

You say you're feeling sleepy.
You say 'Thanks for being there'
You ask me if I'll stay with you,
You feel I really care.

The silences grow longer.
My heart begins to break,
It's really hard not knowing
If, tomorrow you will wake.

You may wake up as normal,
Still wishing you were dead,
Or your parents, they may find you
Still lying in your bed.

Most think the young are happy,
That their future's bright ahead,
But, too many youngsters really feel,
That they wish, that they, were dead.

But we're here for you, we hear your voice,
We'll listen to you cry.
We'll feel your pain together,
As you bid your world, goodbye.

Mary Finnigan

UNTITLED

These people whose lives are so different from ours,
who'd have guessed they would collide,
when things get so bad,
to end it all they finally decide.

We lend an ear, we lend a heart,
and their troubles try to share,
they feel so safe when they're with us,
the only ones who care.

Then at the end, when they have done,
and on their way they go,
what happens then within their lives,
we rarely get to know.

But what we get from doing this,
being a good Samaritan,
is knowing that there is a chance,
they'll decide to carry on.

Mike

HEAVEN INTO HELL

Once again entrapped in my quarters.
These suppressive walls that surround me,
I have pondered a thousand times.

Still I come up with no answers,
With no means of escape.
Instead only ultimate confusion,
And my own personal disrepute.

Nobody comes to visit.
Nobody brings me cigarettes.
All those voices are faceless,
And my feeling is always abject.

The only hope is this window.
But outside it the land is bare.
The only life is a serpent.
It haunts me in my nightmare.

Where is all the colour?
It has gone down with the sun.
Will it ever emerge again?
Only when your time is done.

Here my jealousy develops,
Like an apple on a tree.
Humane and irresistible.
Adam is confused and lonely.

Why have I been burdened with such sensitivity
Is it such an unattractive thing?
Now I have been battered and bruised
By the evil people bring.

And in this hell we live in,
This purgatory brown and bare,
All of us are truly evil;
None of us prepared to care.

But with the future holds hope.
There is one means through the wall.
We shall some day recollect the past,
And will not be divided in the fall.

So come my friends,
Let us break free from these shackles,
We shall be happy again,
Let us rise up against evil
And be reunited as men.

Through the bars a change will appear.
The snake will shed its skin.
All of us will hear
How genesis is going to begin.

Springs will appear.
Fresh water will cover the rock.
There will be streams and rivers
And no more chains or locks.

There will be libation
And ritual pieties.
There will be white garland heifers,
And wines and olive trees.

The red and bare scrubland
Will become filled with life and fecundity.
By the power of unscathed hands
We shall once again be happy.

There will be rain to quench the earth,
The sun will be revealed once more.
Male and female shall live at peace together
And there shall be only natural law.

When this finally happens
We shall be together my friends,
It shall be utopia refound.
Until our heaven once again ends.

Tom Hall

DAY BY DAY

One more day
One more sky
One more cloud
Some more rain
Where is the colour I long for
How things change, how cruel
What's around the corner
Please, no more punches
But what can I do
continue?
Day after day
Night after night
sleepless
I want to break out
I need to be free
Free from my mind
But what can I do
Continue
Keep looking, searching for a way
To smash these chains, rid this weight I carry
To be happy
To live not exist
I long for the sun to shine
to shine and shine and calm my mind
Bright blue skies
Lush green fields
The warm sun that shines and shines.

Julian Clayton Horwell

CARING FOR CALLERS

Samaritans!
Who needs them?
What can they do?
Listen and care?
Tea, make a drink?
Help, learn and think.

Samaritans!
Who are they?
Does anyone know?
Secretive and shy
Are they all saints?
Sorry, can't say.

Samaritans!
Who'll volunteer?
Who will be chosen?
Who will decide?
Who'll man the phone?
Then you're alone.

Samaritans!
What's it about?
First there's the training
Then there's commitment
And fill in the rota:
Rules - it's all rules!

Samaritans!
Who's perfect we rail?
We're human, we try.
What's in it for us?
The reward isn't clear
But note we're still here

Carole

UNTITLED

I pick up the phone and hear someone cry,
Samaritans can I help you?
A whispered voice says I want to die,
Can you tell me why you feel as you do,
and everything you tell me is only between me and you.

The voice says I'm falling apart,
I don't even know where to start,
I say take your time we have got all day,
and I really care about what you have to say.

My name is John Doe the Caller sighs,
can I speak to you without any ties?
Of course you can I reassure,
but I cannot promise I have any cure.

I am so alone and full of fear,
as I have lost someone very dear,
now I am scared as I am all alone,
don't think I can make it on my own.

Forty years we spent together,
always content no matter what the weather,
now she is gone and my heart is sore,
I don't even want to go past my front door.

I know she wouldn't want me to feel this way,
I am only living from day to day,
I am seriously thinking of taking my own life,
so I can be with my darling wife.

A little silence as John catches his breath,
he says he cannot think of anything other than death,
the world seems so grey, and nothing looks real,
it is helping a bit telling you how I feel.

The last two weeks it's felt like hell,
because I've had no one to tell,
all this emptiness deep inside,
I just want to curl up and hide.

I'm beginning to think I might be able to face tomorrow,
knowing I have someone to share my sorrow,
will I be able to call some more?
yes I say and if you like you call at the door.

Colin 23

UNTITLED

Look, dying ain't easy,
But it's a whole lot harder
To go on living.
Sure, it's good to know you care,
But can you give me back my mum,
Can you give me back my childhood
Or my lover
Or my self respect.
I want to feel safe,
I want to lie in someone's warm embrace
And to hear someone tell me
That they love me.
This moment, talking to you,
Is like a harbour.
But I can't be moored up here forever,
And outside these walls
The sea is rough
And people drown.
I never thought dying would be easy,
But I hoped living would be.
Just some of the time.

Fredwyn

KAREN

File the certificate,
close the latest case.
No matter what her name was;
No matter what her face.

It's easy for officials -
They're not required to weep.
They have no dreams to haunt them
And wake them from their sleep.

It is left for those who knew you
to stop and wonder why,
To look inside their inmost thoughts.
Did you really have to die?

Was there some way it was written
On your face or in your speech?
Weren't there any indications?
Was there no way we could reach

Your devastating secret,
Your feeling of despair?
Was there nothing you could tell us?
Nothing we could share?

We must learn to come to terms with
The limits of our power;
Accept the right we all have
To crush our own life's flower;

Honour the choice of others;
Respect their private rights;
Just be there if they need us;
Keep vigil through their nights.

Karen, you have reminded us
Of what we're really all aware -
We are not Gods, but people
Off'ring help by being there.

Howard

UNTITLED

I've seen it all and been through the mill
Weathered the storms with courage and skill
Been down the roads of heartache and pain
Turned right around and gone down them again
Seen bits of life I would rather not share
Taken the paths that lead to nowhere
I've spoken at length or I've kept it all in
Lived for virtue then dabbled with sin
Given my best and dished out the worst
Brought up the rear, been occasionally first
Had things to say some consider as black
Thought better of it and taken them back
Taken some knocks as my shoulders are broad
Sometimes been boring but never been bored
Often thought life like a roller coaster ride
Then seen that the coin has more than one side
Suffered some dirt but come out of it clean
That's what I've done and that's where I've been
This is my life, I am what you see
Will I be of use if a caller rings me?
I could talk for as long and as hard as the rest
But ask me to listen and I'll do my best
Let me hear what you need to tell
I'll try my hardest to do it well
I know who I was and you know who I am
Do I have what it takes to be a good Sam?

Alex

PAIN

Sharp, rending
Mind bending
Heart rending
Never ending
Pain

Knife cutting
Head butting
Soul gutting
Door shutting
Pain

Fingers pointing
Disjointing
Voices taunting
Others flaunting
Pain

Dark descending
No-one tending
Life offending
Ache attending
Pain

Phone ringing
Ear listening
Comfort bringing
Hope winging
No more
Pain

Pam

NEVER TOO LATE

Beautiful death beckons me.
With her welcoming fingers stretching towards me
her comforting blackness is oozing this way.

Swallow me whole.
Protect me; like an innocent child let me curl in a ball
And surround me with your black ignorance

My mind is in chaos
A never ending struggle of gargoyles
All my problems are demons
Laughing as I strain
to contain them.

And she's coming hearer
Death's heartbeat is booming
Closer and closer
Not so lovely now?
Not so safer?
An urgency drives her to take me.

I'm afraid, I'm afraid
In this pitiful place
Can you reach me?
Can you touch my fingers?
Hold onto my hand
And pull me, try to grasp me?
Don't let me slip
Death's black hole is beneath me!

I'm afraid, I'm so scared
She's pulling my toes
Downwards, and clasping my ankles
Can you talk to me? *Talk to me!*
Can you help me? Please?

Julie

IS SOMEONE THERE?

I need a friend
Is someone there?
I need some help
I'm in despair.
The time has come,
I can't go on.
Oh, hear my plea,
I need someone.

Now come, my dear
Pick up the phone
We'll let you see
You're not alone.
We want to help
That's why we're here.
So please do tell
Me of your fear.

It's past midnight
I'm very cold.
I want to die,
I'll grow not old.
Just stay with me
And help me through
Don't pull me back
I beg of you.

Please tell me all
Lest you decide
To take the path
Of suicide.
It is your right
I can't deny.
Who will you leave
Behind to cry?

I didn't think
About my son,
And he is not
the only one.
I'll try again,
You give me hope.
I'll find the strength,
I'll try to cope.

I took this call,
The minutes went.
We talked and talked,
And now I'm spent.
A life is saved
And just in time.
Thank God she called
The Samaritan line.

Maureen

LOVE TOO LATE

My friend took flowers and left them at your gate
With other blossoms there, to venerate
A small sad life which knew no happiness.
Did you know comfort from the soft clean rain
Which gently fell to try erase the sorrow
And wash away tears shed for no tomorrow?
No arms to hold you loving and secure
No warm contentment and no mother near.
Abuse, neglect, hate; feelings stemmed from strife,
All these you knew in thirteen years of life.
Were you conceived in love? Why were you born?
To slip away in death, for us to mourn?
My friend took flowers and left them at your gate
As though in some small way to compensate
For all your grief and pain -
A love too late.

Nancy

A QUESTION OF SUICIDE

She dialled the number in final despair
Just to hear someone speak, her aloneness to share.
'Can I help you, it's the Samaritans here.'
The voice that answered was quiet and clear.

She was feeling numb, but her hold was tight
On the telephone life-line, her knuckles white.
That voice again, 'Take your time, there's no hurry,
'We're always here. You don't have to worry.'

She struggled to speak, but the words wouldn't come.
Still she clung to the phone, (tho' silent and dumb.)
As she stared at the bottles, the papers and bills
That cluttered the table, she picked up the pills.

'It's too late' she whispered 'This must be the end,
I can't carry on why to pretend?'
Her voice started to break, at last tears could start
To ease her anguish; sobs (rent) her apart.

The voice came softly again in reply,
'I'm here to listen, maybe you could try
To tell me about it. We're quite alone,
Only you and me at the end of the phone.'

The minutes passed as she tried to tell
In stumbling words of her private hell.
It wasn't easy, the pauses were long
In the tragic story of what had gone wrong.

Well into the night the Samaritan shared
Her misery and pain. Someone really cared.
Someone sympathised, seemed to understand
And be there beside her, quite close at hand.

Perhaps now with a friend who'd support her, be there,
She could face one more day, endure the despair.
At least for tonight the crisis had passed.
She put down the phone. Then sleep came at last.

June

WHAT WILL I DO

What will I do when the rent falls due
What will I do when I need new shoes
What will I do when I've no money to eat
What will I do when I'm thrown on the street

What will I do when birthdays arrive
What will I do when all my friends die
What will I do when I've nowhere to go
What will I do with no job or home

What will I do when there's silence all round
What will I do when no help can be found
I pick up the phone for a welcoming sound
And talk to some people who are always around

They don't have answers, or think they know best
They never make judgements, or say, 'Do this next'
They give me some time, and a listening ear
And show some support for this man who's in tears . . .

Frank

VERSES OF GRIEF

I am a sad Samaritan
Who tired to write a verse
To give voice to my feelings
As I drove behind the hearse.

I couldn't find a rhythm
To express my grief and pain,
I couldn't make it rhyme or scan
My efforts were all vain.

You can't put great big feelings
Into a little place;
The wild disordered uncontrolled
Won't fit a structured space.

I can't express my misery
In a structured, patterned rhyme.
My loss, my heartbreak and my tears
Need far more space and time.

Yet that is what I have to do:
Shape this torment to my heart;
Let love remembered quench regret;
Let the healing process start.

Mandy

UNTITLED

I thought I'd be a hero
Take a course or read a book
On how to save a life
With clever words and knowing look

I thought that I could turn you
Pull you up and make you think
Of life's forgotten treasures
Lead you gently from the brink

But life is not so rosy
And death *does* have its domain
And who's to say you're right or wrong
Who's mad or who is sane?

So I sit here in your darkness
Which I'm powerless to light
Powerless to see beyond
Powerless to fight
Powerless to find the words
To say to pull you through

All I can do is listen
The choice belongs to you

Penny

BEING THERE

I felt afraid and could tell no one
I felt alone and no-one cared.

Why won't they mention his name?
I want to talk about him
I need to remember
but my friends ignore him
change the subject
death embarrasses them.

I felt afraid and could tell no-one
I felt alone and no-one cared.

The sun is shining
but it's light can't
penetrate the blackness
nothing matters
there is no future
I can't go on.

I felt afraid and could tell no-one
I felt alone and no-one cared.

I found talking painful
it didn't matter
the voice was gentle
the silence soothing
you waited until
I was ready to speak

I felt afraid and someone listened
I felt alone and someone cared.

Denise

THE SHARING

A Samaritan . . . *Me*?
Surely this could never be
you out there
me in here
just voices in-between
how could you ever hope to lean
on such as me to share
your problems
hurt confusion
pain and yes
your dark despair?

You called
and calling made me see
that this perhaps was meant to be
you somewhere
me still here
between us just a sigh
and at your final calm goodbye
I marvelled it was true
you said it helped to lean on me
when friend
I'd leant on *You!*

Yet many times I question still
and guess maybe I always will.

Rita (Leeds)

3.00 AM

you paint despair
ebon-blue
& grief
magenta
yet isolation is a jet
black night

and in my echo
shall only your voice sing

your words
stuff with brine
& curve the air
of a fractured ocean
yet let its sirens
not seduce

and in my echo
shall only your voice sing

you dance with ghosts
burn ash on your forehead
a soul
laid bare
yet life thrums
insistent

and in my echo
shall only your voice sing

you pierce the mask show me
hollow eyes
& the dark
eclipses your mind
yet the coin of night must
spin with day

and in my echo
shall only your voice sing

Gill

HOPE DIES

When death raised its hooded head and
revealed its twisted face
Twined with an infinite time of sorrow,
hope died.
Now, bubbling life away in a false array of smiles
and laughter
But living, contained.
In a fragile egg, laid by despair.
And inside the brightly coloured, shining shell
despair's offspring grows,
until its size becomes overpowering for the thin
shell to contain
The shell, with life, crack is
spewing forth its putrid contents,
Flooding life
Blurring reality
And the whole life slips from its balancing perch
into eternal blackness.

Thomas

I WILL NEVER KNOW

You rang,
I answered
You wanted to talk
I listened.
You were hesitant at first,
I tried to be patient
You told me your worries,
I tried to be understanding
You told me what made you upset
I tried to be sympathetic
You shared your life with me,
I shared my time with you
You thanked me
But did I really help?
Where are you now?
Are you happy now?
Did I help?
I will never know.

Heather

FIRST CALL

FIRST CALL . . . A NEW P'S PANTOUM

To-day I will take my first call
My hands are all clammy and cold,
And this morning I'm not on the ball
I've forgotten all I've been told.

My hands are all clammy and cold
Though my tutor's here at my side.
Will I ever fit in the Sam mould?
Will I know when to moot suicide?

Though my tutor's here by my side
Suppose it's a warning of bombs
I'm not very certain inside
Of the sex calls, or threatening tones.

Suppose it's a warning of bombs
Some callers are not what they seem
I must not let my brain go all numb
For my tutor and I make a team.

Some callers are not what they seem
And this morning I'm not on the ball
But my tutor and I make a team
So, to-day I will take my first call.

Mel 120

THE FIRST CALL

On my first Samaritan duty, awaiting calls with apprehension
Sipping endless cups of coffee, trying to hide my nervous tension.
Training sessions long completed, observation duties past
Reassuring smile from Leader, I can take a call at last.

Soon the telephone is ringing, when I answer will I cope?
All at once the tension passes, I'm relaxed and full of hope.
First the sobbing, then the silence. 'Take your time, no need to hurry
Be assured it's confidential, we won't tell so please don't worry'.

Soon the story starts unfolding, long kept secrets pouring out
'Was it me who caused the conflict?' Plagued by guilt and full of doubt.
Memories of unhappy childhood, father shouting, mother's screams,
Cringing fearful in the bedroom. 'These past terrors haunt my dreams'

Gradually the voice seems calmer, confidence returns at last.
Wonder why my back is aching, notice that an hour has past.
'Yes, I did feel suicidal, when I told of family strife
Whilst you listened there in silence. Now I feel there's more to life.'

'When will you be next on duty? I was fearful what you'd say
But you quietly reassured me, coaxing all my fears away.
It is clear you're so experienced by the way you took my call.
Not surprising, on reflection. You're Samaritans after all.'

Salopian

THE FIRST CALL

'She's dead you know', a voice at last,
'She's gone . . . no future . . . just the past,
there's nothing left, no need to live . . .
so tired . . . nothing left to give . . . '
Then silence, should I speak or not?
I must give space, she needs a lot.
No sound, no tears just silent pain,
I need to speak . . . but must refrain.
It seems like hours and then I say,
'It's alright I'm here . . . I won't go away,
just take your time, no need to rush',
no answer . . . just a desperate hush.
Emotion flowing down the line,
I'm feeling hers . . . is she sensing mine ?
Will she trust me will she speak ?
Was I too forceful? She seems so weak.
Another age is passing by,
And then I hear a quiet cry . . .
So stifled . . . fighting . . . won't let go,
Tears of sadness, tears of woe . . .
'My baby's dead . . . I can't go on . . .
I want to go where she has gone . . .
I want to sleep and feel no pain . . .
I want my baby back again.'
She's letting go, it's flooding out,
she wants to scream and cry and shout,
with fear and guilt and anger too,
so frightened of what she could do.
She talks, I listen, and slowly then . . .
she tells of a daughter, aged nearly ten,
so pretty, kind and good was she,
off to school full of mischief and glee,
never to return, not that day or any . . .
killed on the road with her best friend Jenny.

I say all the things that my training permits,
I'm finding it hard, just keeping my wits,
trying not to let go of the emotion I feel,
this isn't my training . . . this role-play is real.
The call lasts an hour but it seems more like three,
when the caller is gone, it's back to just me . . .
No movement or words . . . just deep, deep despair . . .
I look to my left . . . and my partner is there.
She looks in my eyes and immediately knows,
that it starts in my head, and goes down to my toes.
I'm drained and confused, did I help. No or yes?
What will happen to the caller? I can't even guess . . .
The support I receive is a wonderful thing . . .
She lets me unload . . . takes me under her wing.
It eases my worries and confronts hidden fears,
just to talk through my feelings, both with laughter and tears . . .
So I'm over the hurdle, I've taken a call . . .
I'm really quite short, but just now I feel tall . . .
I know I can do it . . . my confidence grows,
but who is the next caller ? . . .
That . . . nobody knows . . .

Julie 967

FIRST NIGHT
(NIGHT THOUGHTS)

The cold night stretches out ahead
I wonder should I go to bed
Or sit here by the telephone?
This is the first night on my own.

My nerves are stretched taut as a string
I wonder what the night will bring
Who will it be. How will I cope
If it is someone without hope?

My heart starts racing at this thought
And confidence slides down the (slippery) slope
Come on. You must be in control
If you are going to help at all.

The 'phone! The ringing makes me leap
It almost brings me to my feet
Calm down. You must appear composed
Breathe deeply, now here goes.

Those five words helped *me* in some way
The training has begun to pay
My ear hurts. I must learn not to press
The telephone when under stress.

How did it go. Was I all right.
Was she aware of my own fright?
I wish I'd said - but it's too late
To think new things. To speculate

A new day dawns, the sun appears
Wiping away the dark nights fears
I step into my other life
But for others, only strife.

Doug

NIGHT CALLS

A FRIEND IN THE NIGHT

It's been a bad day with the wind and the rain,
Colleagues at work just pass the blame,
Getting dusk now, someone puts on the light
They can't wait to get home where they know it's alright.
But what of the folks who live alone,
Seldom see anyone, to whom can they moan?
They have the same feelings, but alas they can't share
Their frustrations or dreams - does anyone care?
The telephone rings, I feel anxious too,
But lift up the phone,
Samaritans, can I help you?
Only a sob can I hear in the night,
Someone is breaking their heart, poor mite.
Gently I speak and tell them to cry,
I'll not put the phone down
I'm their friend in the night.
The call may last for an hour or so,
Or just a few minutes, we really don't know.
But if we can listen to somebody's plight,
And with words simple can show there is light.
The crying has stopped and their burden is eased,
I know that my duty tonight makes me pleased.
Morning is here, another new day,
I'm off to work now, what can I say?
The sun it is shining, the sky's a light blue,
I'm glad to be back working with you.
A smile here and there and everyone's bright,
What's brought this on?
My duty last night.

Arthur

HIS FIRST TIME!

He turned in his sleeping bag for the umpteenth time in the night
Picking up the telephone to make sure it was working all right
After all it was his first night duty in a room all on his own
And he was nervous in case he missed the ring of the telephone
The phone rang, he went to answer it quickly, thinking what to say
No, don't answer immediately, let it ring awhile that's the correct way
He then picked up the phone, 'Samaritans', then he heard the click
Oh dear receiver replaced, why, was he too slow or maybe too quick
Did his voice sound nervous or maybe lacking in confidence
Maybe the caller didn't understand, it was so quick it didn't make sense
He did feel annoyed with himself, but maybe he was not to blame
After all the phone was replaced and he'd only said the Samaritan name
He still felt guilty perhaps they wanted to talk about a problem they had
On thinking this his feeling of guilt turned to making him feeling sad
He lay in his sleeping bag, looked at the phone willing it to ring
Nothing happened, he stared so long his eyes began to sting
Closed his eyes to rest them so when it did ring he would be alert
It rang again, but the same thing happened, he felt quite hurt
Was it his voice, did he sound caring enough, was he doing it wrong
Next time it rings he would sound confident, hope it will not be too long
But the same thing happened four or five times during the night
What was he doing wrong, he must concentrate and get it right
The phone rang, he answered it fully not hearing a click
Perhaps this time he could be of help, his heart gave a skip
Is that the Samaritans? Yes, would you like to speak to me?
No, I rang up because I really want to speak to a young lady!

David

UNTITLED

Every night she seems to ring
On and on, the same old thing
We have heard it all before
She's becoming quite a bore.

But there must be something more
So I turn it all about
Change the subject, change the score
Slowly then, it all comes out
Things we've never heard before
From dark corners of her mind
Pour guilty secrets from her youth
Until now she could not find
Now the bitterness of years
Is suddenly dissolved in tears.

'I feel unworthy, dirty, cheap
Had I the will.
I have the pills
To find oblivion in sleep
Thanks for being so polite
And understanding, now, Goodnight'.

A sigh, a click, and she is gone
Thoughtfully, I climb in bed
And lie silent and alone
Her fears and doubts now fill my head
Will she do it?
She has tried
Once before and
Nearly died.

Worried, anxious, did I fail?
I tried my best, but even so
Was it all to no avail?

Maybe we shall never know.

Wilfred

THE NIGHT WATCH

The phone rings - a voice speaks

S tutteringly?
A pprehensively?
M iserably?
A nxiously?
R oughly?
I ndecently?
T rustingly?
A pologetically?
N onchlantly?
S oftly?

We strain to listen, anxious not to miss
the inward tear
the suicidal fear
the wistful note of longing for a
sympathetic ear

And as we answer - the dawn breaks

Elsie (Torquay Branch)

NIGHT DUTY

It's been a busy night with constant calls.
At half past three I hadn't been to sleep;
And then a lull - I must have slept at once.
From somewhere deep I heard the phone again;
Five minutes could have passed, or half an hour,
I'd no idea; I just felt tired and cold.
The voice was scared. 'Oh, good, there's someone there.'
'We're here. I'm Christine. Would you like to talk?'
'No. Now I know you're there I'll be all right.'
Oh - she's rung off; I made a mess of that,
Waking like that I wasn't at my best.
I hope I didn't sound unwelcoming.
I said my name too soon - I should have tried
To get her talking about why she rang.

I haven't slept, and now it's getting light.
She sounded scared - I hope she'll be all right.

I'm glad I rang. I think I'll make some tea.
I didn't think there'd be a *person* there,
I thought it would be one of those machines.
I'm glad she said her name - she sounded nice,
But I can't talk to anybody yet.
I've got to concentrate to stay intact;
If I let go, my mind will fall to bits.
I felt so frightened - it was all so quiet -
I thought I was the only person left.
- I'm in the kitchen. Why aren't I in bed?
Oh, I remember, I was making tea.
Here are my tablets; passport to escape.
It keeps me going, knowing that they're there.
It's lucky that I'm good at swallowing pills.
How many would I need? I've got a lot;
Plenty, I think, but I won't take them yet.
I'll drink my tea, then I'll go back to bed.

I haven't slept, but now it's getting light.
I've managed to hang on for one more night.

Christine

THE NIGHT CALLER

When semi shadows of
the day
turn into spectres of
the night
the torment in my mind
spreads out its tentacles;
and the pressure of
four walls lean on
my despair and
I panic
with the fading of
the light.

And,
as I sink into a
pit of self-destruction,
I reach out for a number
so well-known
and I hear the friendly voice
which will sustain me
through the terrors of
a night
both wide and long.

Pamela

ON NIGHT DUTY

I am here

Loud and urgent the telephone
through the silent, rainy night.
Unseen faces, lonely homes,
broken hearts in squalid places.
Voices needing, searching;
voices, crying, screaming;
'Are you there? Can you hear?'
- Yes, my friend, yes I am here -

Like a flickering distant light
at the silent, vigil harbour
where dreams and feelings
tossed and shattered gather;
deep the sorrow, deep the anger,
long the night, no hope in sight.
'Do you know how I feel? Do you care?'
- Yes I know. Yes I care

The rain against the window pane
while a trembling voice asks my name.
'Help me come' he says and then
all the excuses and the abuses.
'I can't sleep! I want a shag,
so talk me through as I hold my Jack.
Are you there? Are you near?'
- Yes I am here, but not for that! -

And as I wonder why I stay
I hear a whisper: 'I've taken tablets,
I've reached the end, I want to die.
I have no friends. No one will cry.
Don't ask my name, just talk to me
and as I die, please pray for me
Are you there? Can you hear?'
- Yes, I am here, hold on, I am here.

You are the reason why I am here.

Carrie Jones

UNTITLED

I pick up the phone and say hello
I'm Robert and I'm a Sam
Talk to me and tell me what's wrong
And I'll listen as best I can

Your distress is real, you're saying what you feel
And you're feeling bad right now
But tell me and I'll listen
Perhaps it will help somehow

It's an overnight and it's 2am
And I'm feeling tired and low
I'd love to sleep but I guess it'll keep
Cos the phone will ring I know

I don't have a cure
I can't make it right
I can't wave a magic wand
But by talking to me perhaps you'll see
That somehow life can go on

Robert K

THOUGHTS IN THE SMALL HOURS

The darkest hour precedes the dawn
The brightest Sam's not at his best,
Yet often that's when trouble's born
And gives the Sam the strongest test.

The Sam could gladly fall asleep,
The caller cannot and could well
Opt for a longer form of rest
Because he feels his life is hell

Listen with kindness, be aware,
Don't give advice but do try hard
To let him know you really care;
That you at least do not disdain
His inarticulate cry of pain

Did you succeed? You'll never know
He put the phone down yet you got
A certain feel, a kind of sense,
The way he talked, that he will not . . .

Is it worthwhile, the training days,
The early rising, long tired nights:
The hours spent sitting by a phone
With better things to do at home?

Sex calls, time wasters on the line
Thinking it fun to take your time:
All so that one in genuine need
May feel there's someone who will heed.

Just waiting for a call to come
Counts little in the world's great sum.
Can you by such a simple thing
Really contribute anything?

Each day a million lives are lost
By cruelty, famine, greed and war;
The careless driving of a car.
By how much then to count the cost
Of one more life among the rest:
Is there some litmus paper test?

Just as your caller must decide
Whether to take his life or live,
So you must in the end assess
The worth of what you have to give.

The widow's mite was very small
And yet it counted over all.

Eric

OVERNIGHT

Ten o'clock. Time to go.
Grudgingly, grumblingly. Cold outside.
Bed beckons, warm and welcoming.
Not for me; not tonight.
Ah well, who cares.

Eleven o'clock,
'Samaritans, can I help you?
Of course it doesn't matter
That you've had a few. I'll listen.'
Oh God, a drunk!
Why do I always get the drunks;
Why can't they realise that they're incomprehensible?
Please go to sleep or drop the phone.
Oh dear, he has!
Ah well, who cares.

Midnight. A call.
Silence; then sobbing softly.
Few words. The question's asked.
The answer's 'Yes'
'Please try to talk.
No, please don't go.'
Too late; she's gone.
Ah well, who cares.

Half past one. You're back.
I'm glad you called again.
All I can do is be with you,
Be sad with you, be glad with you;
I'll cry with you, and try with you,
And share your hopes and fears with you,
Until the pain has passed.

Eight o'clock. Time for home.
A shave, a shower,
And feeling human once again.
It's over. Till the next time.
Ah well, who cares.

I suppose I must,
If I was there, the night you needed me.

Martin

NIGHT LINE

Time-stretchers, we are here again
in case: moon shadows, coffee grouts,
the suppressed screams of telephones:
I am hearing voices, straining,

insubstantial, spaced-out, bereft
of loved and loathed familiars,
trapped in the yawning hours, tiring
of time, of whatever is left

before they're done: nightmares, night lines,
life lines. Still it is a question
of seeing things through. Day may break
the spell.

Colin

SILENT CALLS

THE SILENT CALLER

'Samaritans - can I help you?'

'You sound distressed, it's alright, take your time'
Get her confidence, please let her be fine.

'Can you manage to tell me what is wrong?'
She's falling apart, for her please stay strong.

'My name is Anita, do you want to tell me yours?'
She can't tell me, perhaps she needs a quiet pause.

'I'm still here, no of course I'll not go away'
Careful don't panic her with wrong thing to say.

'Is it that you are feeling suicidal, It's OK to cry'
Please let me help you, or at least let me try.

'I'll stay on the line quietly, and give you some space'
Still silent, sobbing, if only I could see her face.

'Hello, hello! What's happened are you still there?'
I hope I have conveyed just how much I care.

'I'm still listening, Oh no you've put down the phone'
Please God let her realise she is not alone.

Anita

CARING IN SILENCE

Samaritans, can I help you?
Hello, are you still there?
Can you tell me how you are feeling
Are you frightened being out there?

I'm still hanging on to listen,
Are you finding it so hard to say
Why you're feeling so sad and abandoned
On another grey, miserable day?

I shall not put the phone down, don't worry,
I am here till you need me no more,
You need not be alone with your troubles
I shall listen and not close the door.

Would you like me to carry on talking
Or would quietness help you to think?
Can I help you to answer the question -
Do you feel that your life's on the brink?

I can hear that you're quietly weeping,
Can I reach out and offer my care?
May I put my arm round your shoulders
Let you know that there's somebody there?

Oh, OK, you want to be leaving -
Yes, I'm glad that I was here, too,
Please call back when you feel you are able,
I'll be here with my time, just for you

Suzi

THE LISTENER

'Samaritans, can I help you?'

Your sobbing fills my ear.
Immediately I am touched by your deep heart rending sobbing.

'You're through to the Samaritans now,
can I help you?'

Your weeping fills me with such concern,
and I want to hold you and comfort you.
Stay on the line.

'Just take your time. It's alright,
I'm not going anywhere.'

You are out there, amid the turbulent sea of humanity,
I feel the lonely despair of your solitary heart drowning,
and your weeping melts me with compassion.

'It's alright, I'm still here for you'

Our lives have touched,
You have reached out to the one willing to be caught,
If only you knew that I am vulnerable too,
Yet at this moment you are the most important factor in my life.
Now your despair is mine.
Yet can I not reach beyond your tears?

'Would you like to try and tell me what is upsetting you so much?'

Trust me.
Share your sorrow with me.
Hold onto the lifeline that you have dialled,
and let me lead you to a safer hold.

'I know it's difficult to talk, you sound so upset,
I would like to try to help you.'

Who are you?
Where are you?
Why such pain?
Hold onto this line,
Tell me how you're feeling,
Your despair is so deep,
Can you yet be helped?

'You sound so unhappy
are you thinking about ending your life?'

Click,
Silence.

'How was your caller Mary?'

'I don't know, there was just weeping,
I hope the caller rings back.'

Mary

SILENT CALL

'Samaritans, can I help?' The gentle voice,
and on the telephone, only background noise.

'Is there something you want to talk about?
Has something happened today?'
'I'm hurting deep, I cannot speak.'
The background noise just says.

'How do you feel, can you let me know?
Can you tell so I can care?'
But all the while the silence cries,
As background sounds we share.

'Is the pain so bad, you want to die?'
'So bad you can't explain,
How going on is just too much?'
The background hums remain.

The silence stretches on a while,
and then the phone goes down.
Was it enough to hear a voice,
Amongst the background sounds?

'Samaritans, can I help?' the caring, gentle voice,
and on the telephone again, there's only background noise.

Alan

SILENCE IS GOLDEN?

Are you listening to this deep, dark silence
Broken only by racking sobs?
Can you feel beyond the abyss
Into this turmoil of deep despair?

I wish you could see this shattered wreck
That cannot think, that cannot speak.
I wish you could see beyond the 'phone
Into the darkened torments of my mind.

I've let you down - I should have talked
But all I can do is cry again.
I'm so choked up that words won't come
And tortuous silence screams at my soul.

Speak, oh speak, why can't I speak?
Only a few words - if only I could.
Please can you see beyond the sobs
To the words I'm trying to say?

Kathy (Cambridge)

MY SILENT CALLER

The phone rings, the air is engulfed with a sense of apprehension,
I pick up the receiver, I feel the tension.

'Samaritans, can I help you?' I say in a gentle tone,
To let the caller know that they are not alone.

A few seconds elapse, it feels like a lifetime,
Is there anyone there at the end of the line?

I softly repeat 'Can I help you at all?'
The phone crashes down, they've ended the call.

The phone rings, the same thing happens again,
Are they unable to talk, unconscious, in pain?

Is my voice not suitable, too unfriendly, too cold?
Has the idea of death taken too firm a hold?

The phone rings once more, its piercing ring,
I pick up the receiver, exactly the same thing.

Have I failed in my duty as a Samaritan volunteer?
Can I do any more than simply be here?

Once more the phone rings out loud and clear,
Once more the caller doesn't talk, is it shame, is it fear?

Is it a sex caller wasting my time?
Is it some crank hogging the line?

The rings appear louder as the phone goes once more,
'Samaritans, can I help you?' - a quiet voice replies 'Well I'm not sure'.

I've phoned a few times but the words wouldn't come out,
'Just take your time,' I say, 'Try and tell me what it's all about'.

Slowly, he finds courage and a painful picture begins to unfold,
Of events that took place but never before told.

I listen, he talks, he has a sad story to tell,
One I've heard before and know only too well.

The hours pass by and my call comes to an end,
He thanks me for being there, for being a friend.

As I sit by the phone and await my next call,
I think maybe I'm not such a bad Samaritan after all.

Joan

UNTITLED

This silence on the phone
You ring
But there is only silence.
A mask for you,
A wilderness for me.
How I long for the click drone
That ends this silence
On the phone.

Tony

IN THE SILENCE

Listen
    Listen
        Listen
Can you hear
the silent claim
and feel the broken heart,
- a speck of hope sustain?
Seize it
cusp its flame
protect its fading light
    through the night
        and into dawn

until the day takes over.

Alan

THANK YOU

SOPHIE'S STORY

Samaritans? I want to talk
To someone now, before I go.
Can you help? I don't need help.
But you will listen? That is good.
Well, here I am at home again
With four blank walls - I sold the house -
And Munch's painting of The Scream
In front of me as I walk in.
Why is it here? That's how I feel
Just screaming, screaming, inside me
Every long, protracted day.
We were fine 'til we came here,
Living, working in the town.
'Let's pack it in and move,' he said,
'The countryside is fresh and clean.'
All that traffic on the road
But not a bump before we came;
Then in this fresh, clean countryside
A skid, a wall, a crash - the end!
Oh he's alright - he always wins -
No worries now - not in the grave!
I'm left behind to struggle on.
Who wants a cripple on two sticks?
My parents? Brother? What's the use?
They have their problems without mine.
'Hi Mum, Hi Dad, I'm fine' I say.
I have another mother now -
You call it Mother's Ruin - gin!
Well yes, I drink to drown my grief.
Oh yes, I've thought of suicide -
My life is hard but death is sweet.
So am I sure? Of course I'm sure;
I've planned it well, you must admit;
Three chemist's shops in three small towns:
'Some aspirins, please, the largest size.'

And now I have them -
Drink, the gas-fire and my pills.
So, dear Samaritan, good-bye.
You'd like to talk a little while?
You'll stay with me throughout the night?
You wouldn't try to trace my call
But if I like you'll phone me back?
Do I really want to die?
No-one has asked me that before.
I keep it bottled up inside.
Can I see no hope at all?
I haven't thought too far ahead.
It's strange but now I've talked to you
The future seems to be more clear.
But no, I've planned it all, you see:
Tonight is my last night on earth.
Samaritans could keep in touch
Until I'm on my feet again?
And after, if I'm still alone?
It is the loneliness that hurts.
Do I really want to die?
What other option do I have?
It seems to be the only way
To stop this aching void inside.
And yet I'm having second thoughts
Now that I know that you are there
Just one short life-line call away.
Thank you Samaritans, it has helped
To know so many of you care.
Perhaps I might pick up the threads
With your support, one step each day.

Wendy 29

HELP!

I am so sad and in distress,
My life is in a total mess
Family and friends can't help me either
I feel I can't really talk to neither

I'm so mixed up, nothing's clear
Sometimes I wish I wasn't here.
Maybe if I should take a walk,
I'd find someone to whom I could talk,

I saw a sign upon a wall
If you need help just give us a call
24 hours we're always there
You talk, we'll listen, we really care

I phoned the number
she gave no advice
I talked and talked she was really nice;

She helped me through it,
Said they're always there.
To listen to my problems
They really cared.

I'm always grateful to that unknown face
No questions asked about name or place
If you're in a crisis phone their line
Because the ear on the end
Could now be mine.

Chris 16

BEGINNING

I thought about it long and hard
I wanted so to do it
They really were a needed thing
To just be there, should people ring

To be so down - have nothing
No-one to share your troubled thoughts
To be at ease and free to share, with a disembodied voice
Must surely help a lot . . .

. . . I held the phone, and dialled
It was easy, I just got through
And I heard the voice that answered
Say - *'Samaritans, can I help you?'*

I got a friendly call back
Could I come in for a chat?
Then I saw David and Barbara
And, really, that was that

Of course it took a long while, really, because then I had to wait
For other people to be ready, like me, and to be given a date
What a revelation it all was, but somehow, and yet
It all made sense and came together, presented and helped by the Team on 'Prep'

Cecile

THE CALLER

A wretched man phoned the Samaritans
but found it hard to speak
He moved his lips in silent cries
and tears ran down his cheeks.

My name is John the Samaritan said
could you try to say your name
The man was silent for a while
Then cried out in his pain

Why does no one love me
No one gives a damn
Are they so blind they cannot see
the lonely man I am

I don't really want to die
but what else can I do
My hopes and dreams have gone awry
why bother to see things through

There's no arm around my shoulder
no kiss to set me free
from endless nights of loneliness
and years of misery

John blinked his eyes to clear his vision in
and looked to heaven in petition
what could he say what could he do
to help this brother he barely knew

But then the man spoke once again
through his tears and heartfelt pain
I'm sorry John for troubling you
But I just did not know what else to do

I'll leave you now you've listened well
you've helped me through this time of hell.

Must you go I don't even know your name

Thank you John for being there
            I've felt your warmth and your care
I'll tell you now my name's the same
            just like you they call me John
            That final click and then he'd gone.

Trevor 1076

STRANGER ON THE LINE?

I picked the phone up in my hand . . .
  but would a stranger understand?
Just strangers at the other end -
  could one of them become my friend?
Some friends I'd known for quite a while
  would listen, pat my hand and smile . . .
So how could any stranger give
  the help I'd need to want to live?
Just useless phoning my friend, Dee,
  surrounded by her family;
Another friend was full of joy -
  her interest was her latest boy.
Another thought her troubles worse
  than any I could then rehearse.
My doctor gave me pills to calm -
  and told me they would do no harm,
But every day I felt so ill,
  I'd take at least one extra pill;
And as the church told me to pray,
  I'd pray - and cry, till each new day . . .
Until, one night, I could not bear . . .
  with no one near to hear or care.
I picked the phone up in my hand
  to see could *someone* understand.

I talked - and talked. It did me good.
  I felt this stranger understood;
And soon, I felt my burdens ease -
  the nights brought calm and welcome peace;
A good Samaritan was there . . .
  with soothing voice, with words of care
Until I felt someone, somewhere,
  might also need a friend to share
  the night-time hours - when problems find
    a way to flood the tortured mind . . .
and gratefully I said I'd try
  to cope alone - and said, 'Good-bye'.

So if you find you feel alone
please don't forget . . . pick up the phone.
You'll always find a listening friend
is waiting at the other end.

Rita Woodall

INFORMATION

We hope you have enjoyed reading this book - and that you will continue to enjoy it in the coming years.

If you like reading and writing poetry drop us a line, or give us a call, and we'll send you a free information pack.

Write to

Arrival Press Information
1-2 Wainman Road
Woodston
Peterborough
PE2 7BU.